ECSTASY: Shamanism in Korea

ECSTASY:

Shamanism in Korea

by Alan Carter Covell

HOLLYM INTERNATIONAL CORP.
Elizabeth, New Jersey   Seoul

First published in 1983
by Hollym International Corp.
18 Donald Place
Elizabeth, New Jersey 07208 U.S.A.

Published simultaneously in Korea
by Hollym Corporation: Publishers,
14-5 Kwanchol-Dong, Chongno-Ku,
Seoul, Korea Phone: 735-7554

ISBN: 0-930878-33-7
Library of Congress Catalog Card Number: 83-81487

Printed in Korea

DEDICATION

This book is dedicated to the three greatest influences on my research: the Kwanum from California; the Mountain Tiger of Songni-san; the Taoist Master of the U of H. Lastly, the manuscript is indebted to an IBM Correcting Selectric II, which never once broke under the strain of manifold revisions.

Alan Carter Covell
Seoul

PHOTO CREDITS

All photos used in this book were taken by the author with these exceptions:

(Front Cover) Alan Heyman, Kungmin University faculty, Seoul, took this at Samgak-san's Full Moon Kut, 1982.

(Hyatt *kosa*) Bruno Mattlet, Belgium, shot this at the Hyatt Regency, Seoul, September, 1982

These photos, were contributed by Carole Alexander of The Westin Chosun hotel, Seoul. My sister Carole, in her capacity as PR Director for The Westin Chosun, has provided the pictures from file photos of the *kosa* held there in 1981, and the following in a private capacity:

p. 45 fans upon the altar
p. 52 A manshin smoking four cigarettes
p. 59 A Mountain Spirit shrine on Mt. Samgak
p. 68 Manshin cutting away evil influences
p. 80 Hell painting from Pomun-sa on Cheju Island
p. 82 Ibid.

NOTES ON ROMANIZATION: All Korean words Romanized into English follow the McCune-Reischauer system, with the diacritical marks omitted, except for the word referring to spirit or deity in Shamanism which is rendered as *shin,* its actual sound, rather than *sin,* as that system does. Spellings for Chinese names follow the Wade-Giles system of Romanization.

Foreign words are in italics when first used but usually not thereafter.

CONTENTS

Dust Cover (Front): Korea's premier shamaness, a refugee from North Korea, dances before an altar decked with portraits of spirits to be summoned or invited to attend the rituals. She wears the costume of the Buddhist-type Heavenly Spirit (Chesok) as she dances to music from an hourglass drum, a bamboo oboe and brass cymbals (unseen on the left). The microphone belongs to Korean Broadcasting System, which has recently given increasing attention to the ecstatic performances of the northern type of Shamanism, prevalent in the Seoul area.

Dust Cover (Back): "Called by the spirits" at age five, this child *manshin* easily reaches ecstasy while dancing upon sharpened sword blades. She is presently twelve years old, but would seem to be headed for leadership in the fate of Korean Shamanism during the next century.

Front Flap: A manshin in ecstasy, possessed by the Knife-riding General.

Front Endpaper: Shaman dancers painted on the ceiling of Popchu-sa, Buddhist temple in the Songni Mountain National Park. Though these heavenly musicians owe some of their genesis to the Buddhist concept of angels, the function of these dancers is to placate the shaman roof-beam spirit.

Rear Endpaper: A *manshin* in ecstasy, pressing the blade of a brass knife into her throat. Many actions by Korean shamans indicate that science still can't explain everything, for the author has observed and closely studied several rituals where physical harm should have come to the performer, but has yet to see it happen.

PREFACE

This volume undoubtedly will arouse controversy. Shamanism in Korea, being based on oral tradition, not only has changed with the passage of time but even today varies from region to region, with the skill of the performers and the personal needs of its patrons. Thus every general statement always has many exceptions.

My observations are based on *kuts* given by some of the country's experts, those living in Seoul, many of whom fled North Korea when the Communists moved in. Even these expert professionals differ from individual to individual and also from performance to performance, However, a certain basic core remains, and it is this that I have attempted to explain from the viewpoint of a Westerner interested in religious expression as a key to understanding art and culture. Some *mudang* may fake their state of "possession" or degree of "ecstasy," but I have been fortunate to witness both earnest and inspired shamans, who truly believe that they are interpreting the will of the spirits and expressing the deities' moods, which they communicate to the audience at a *kut*. Every part of every costume and every ritual has a religious significance based on the past.

Alan Carter Covell
Seoul, Korea, Honolulu, and Idyllwild, California
4316, Year of Tangun (檀紀)

SHAMANISM'S SEXUAL CORE: AN INTRODUCTION

"When I started 'dancing on the knives,' while possessed by the Knife-Riding General, my husband divorced me," the pretty young shamaness was saying. "He took our two children and married a younger woman. But I never knew any ecstacy with him—only when I dance and am possessed. . ." This Korean shamaness is not yet forty, attractive, and a college graduate, who has mastered all Korean ecstatic shaman rituals, except the descent into Hell, which is so demanding that only very experienced spirit-mediums will undertake it.

In Korea today, more than 95% of the practicing shamans of the ecstatic tradition are females, while an equal proportion of their customers are also women. This tendency for women to occupy the field almost exclusively is in direct contrast to the ancient Siberian Shamanist heritage from which Korea's ecstatic tradition descends, where males were a larger portion of the shamans. Why should this be true of Korea, when both have the same origins? Is this phenomena related to prehistoric Chinese Shamanism of the first millennium B.C., when the *wu* of the Chou dynasty and Chu kingdom were mostly women, seduced into becoming the mortal lovers of powerful, male spirits as demonstrated by the words of the love songs which survive from this period?

Has Shamanism remained a major religion in Korea (while it has vanished in most industrialized countries) because of some root cause in the sexual mores of Korea itself? Are Korea's gender roles different enough to account for the fact that Shamanism is a still living tradition in Korea, and not simply an anachronistic cultural phenomenon? In spite of more than a mil-

lennium of oppression, has Korean Shamanism survived because it fills a psychological need that is basically sexual in connotation?

Most Shamanist spirits or deities are
males; only a few are acknowledged as
females, these generally being classified as
"grandmother spirits." This helps explain
why the small group of male shamans in
Korea today is almost always transvestite,
performing in womens' costume. (These
men are not homosexuals, but simply take
on feminine attributes in their dance and
costume in order to please the male deities,
whom they must invite to possess them.)

The Siberian tradition in which male
shamans were more numerous than female
ones seems to have been true in early
Korean history. However, as Confucianism
became stronger, queens who ruled in their
own right (*yowang*) ceased to appear, with
only consort queens (*wangbi*) being recorded,
as women began to lose their freedom of
physical movement and social mobility.

In the tenth century, during the reign of
King Songjong (981-997) A.D.), a totally
Confucian-type of education was prescribed
for the upper classes. This channelling of
the Korean intellect through a Confucian
focus only increased with time, so that with
the founding of the Yi dynasty in 1392,
male supremacy (as embodied by the Confucian moral code) was a solidly fixed fact
in Korean life.

As has been mentioned by a number of
historians, Korea became more Confucian
than China itself. This meant that the position of women deteriorated still further,
until women could not inherit property, nor
could they remarry after being widowed
(even if it had been a childhood marriage
and never consummated physically). Gradually upper class women became more and
more restricted to the home, appearing in

天下女將軍

天下大將軍

public only when covered from the crown of the head to the ankles by a long overgarment, as strict as the purdah conditions of Moslem India.

In addition, in the capital, women (of the upper class, what the low classes did was of little concern to the nobility) could not leave their homes until the curfew bell sounded and men were supposed to be off the streets. After the age of seven, no mingling of the sexes was permitted, even among brothers and sisters. The males had their part of the house and the females had their own inner (*anbang*) rooms which could be visited only by the husband and children.

By the time the even stricter Neo-Confucian code had settled firmly in place concerning personal behavior, which designated the wife only as a potential begetter of sons, it is no wonder that the birthrate among the upper classes dropped in many cases. Also, no techniques were known about fertility cycles, or how to excite the onset of the fertile period in the body of the woman, techniques which are understood and practiced in many parts of the world. No wonder ideas arose concerning hurrying the onset of conception, such as masturbating with rocks naturally shaped like a male organ, or sympathetic magic used in prayers in fertility gardens (see page 88). Women would make a pilgrimage to odd-shaped geological formations, there to keep a "100 nights vigil," praying to the Mountain Spirit. (It is more than barely possible that some restless monks from Buddhist temples located near these natural features "impersonated" the Mountain Spirit or his messenger, causing many of these 100 night vigils to end with a successful pregnancy.)

Women were not supposed to enjoy sex, nor even serve as objects of sexual pleasure for their husbands; that role was filled by the *kisaeng*. The kisaeng played the role of entertainer for the Yi dynasty equivalent of the "tired business man," (the court scholar-official) who stood at the upper end of the spectrum of Korean society. The Confucian ethic made the female body something to cover and be ashamed of, the skirt line being reminiscent of those in Victorian England.

The ordinary Korean woman did not expect sexual pleasure and hardly realized what she was missing. However, human passions do seek an outlet. For the lower classes, this release sometimes took on the form of what Westerners might term a nervous breakdown, which would be called in Korean *shinbyong,* or "spirit sickness." The only cure for this was to become a shamaness, taking a "spirit-lover" thus letting the pent-up passions be released through ecstatic singing and dancing. (None of this is meant to sound cynical on the author's part, for it was a pragmatic, unconscious solution to an overpowering, physical need.)

Noble women during the Yi dynasty were not allowed to get this disease. If there was a suspicion that one of the female members of the household was suffering from the spirit illness, she would be killed in one way or another (usually by starvation, while being kept locked away in solitary confinement within the home, or by poison, being forced to drink lye). It would not be thinkable for an upper-class family to suffer the shame of having one of its daughters or daughters-in-law become a "base creature" like a shaman. (The shaman class during the Yi dynasty in Korea was considered in the lowest bracket, with butchers, slaves and prostitutes.)

On Cheju Island the shamans were mostly male. The women there did a great deal more physical work than the norm in Korea

and had more independence and freedom of movement; this resulted in fewer cases of the spirit sickness among them. Today, modern women have more social mobility; also they control the family purse strings. The modern, non-career Korean woman devotes herself to her family, her investments and her husband (when he manages to come home. There are few kisaeng houses left in Korea, but the wine-shop girls now fill that role.)

Nothing in this present arrangement challenges the Korean male to improve his love-making techniques, for the idea that the wife's function is to clean house and bear children still lingers, even among the Westernized college students of today. Times are indeed changing in Korea, but from stories told by most Korean men, their idea of sexual satisfaction is the male orgasm, with very little emphasis on the wishes of the partner.

But when the spirit-sickness calls, it is a physical need stirring the woman, a need that can only be satisfied by surrendering to the guardian spirit, and by ecstatic dancing and singing. Denying the call of the spirits has led to more than one death, for the victim of the disease suffers blinding headaches, muscle pains and vision trouble. If the sickness is conquered once, it often returns again, years later, never going away permanently until the stricken one serves the spirits. Being united with the spirits in ecstasy, gives the Korean female shaman what might be termed a "youthful countenance," for many of them look far younger than their actual age. Most Korean female shamans are married as well, or became shamans after marriage. If this doesn't result in divorce or abandonment, it usually leads the husband into a dependent role, staying as far away from his wife's customers as possible.

America's own outbreak of "witchcraft

fever'' took place during the time when Puritanism held sway in New England. This era, a generally severe one concerning religion, was capped off by the Salem witchcraft trials. Women with ''hot tempers,'' or ''improper church attending habits,'' who ranged in age from the thirties to sixties, were accused by a group of teen-age and pre-teen girls as being witches. The general hysteria at the time concerning the devil and his works served to see a number of the accused women hanged as witches.

The Puritan dress code and attitudes towards one's duty to God, were similar to the Confucian dress code and the duty to family relationships. Both treated women as second-class citizens, the Puritans showing their true nature by defining the size of the stick which a husband could use to beat his wife. Both Confucians and Puritans treated sex as vulgar, only necessary for procreation; the principle difference was that Confucians considered the male orgasm important, while the Puritans ignored or condemned it.

A Korean folktale describes how students of the two greatest Confucian scholars of the Yi dynasty (Yulgok and Toegye), anxious to learn from their masters in every way, therefore secretly observed their bedroom behavior. Yulgok ''quietly proceeded to complete the ritual as though he were performing a sacred duty.'' Toegye's pupils were shocked to observe their master in various poses and antics. When they confronted the master the next day, he explained: ''All things obey the laws of nature. My good friend Yulgok will not have posterity. The sky blackens, thunder rolls, lightning flashes and raindrops fall. Then the earth is again filled with plants.'' The tale ends with the remark that Toegye, dead for 500 years, has ''an army of descendants numerous enough to fill a county, while

Yulgok's direct line has long since come to an end."

Until there is a basic change in the attitudes towards the sexual roles of males and females in Korea, the symptoms of shin-byong will probably continue to manifest themselves. The phenomenon of sub-Arctic Shamanism has often been argued to be a type of "Arctic madness," caused by psychotic breaks and the self-healing process, all principally due to the especially severe survival conditions near the Arctic Circle. The weather in Korea, not being nearly as oppressive as that of northern Siberia, leaves no room for the Arctic Madness, so the cause of the shaman sickness must be something equally oppressive to its principal victims, women. The only thing which approaches the severity of oppression which is produced by Arctic weather is that of the blatant sexual repression practiced in ancient (and some ways modern) Korean society.

PART I

SHAMANISM IN ACTION

In this Yi Dynasty painting, a family can be seen hurrying to a kut, the wife with a plate of offerings, while the husband carries the pig in front and his son on his back.

1 KOREA'S ECSTATIC TRADITION

Universality

Since time immemorial, ordinary persons have been intrigued by unusual human beings who achieve altered states of consciousness, those who appear to leave their regular body and travel to other realms to become possessed by supernatural forces—call it "ecstasy," "trance," "prophetic vision," "hypnosis" or whatever, depending on type and degree. Prehistoric humans bestowed special reverence on those among their number who apparently were psychic and departed from the everyday world to communicate with supra-natural "spirits" and return later with messages.

In pre-modern times each area of the planet developed its own group of human intermediaries who flew (spiritually if not literally) between two worlds, that of the living and the other world inhabited by spirits. In Siberia the term for these communicators with special abilities is *saman*; in Indonesia it's *bomoh*: in Malaysia it's *hala*; in Hawaii the spirit-priest is called *kahuna*; all American Indian tribes have their particular "medicine man", such as the *wabeno* for the Chippewa. *Miko* prophesied for the Japanese Shintoists and the Oracle of Delphi was famous in the classical world of Greece.

Dominance

Exquisitely crafted works of art testify to Shamanism's dominance in the Far East in very early times. Among the most spectacular artifacts from Korea's ancient past are the fifth and sixth-century golden crowns and earrings excavated from Silla-period tombs. In China's Anyang tombs, dated around 1500 B.C., Shang-dynasty bronze vessels are generally ranked as the most dazzling of China's ancient artifacts. Both

Musee Guimet crown, a reflection of Korea's Siberian shaman heritage.

art forms were created for the elite of each country, which was practicing a type of Shamanist ritual, with offerings to the spirits; the riches of the state were used for burials of shaman-kings in both early China and early Korea. In each country, animals were endowed with magical powers from which humans sought to benefit by depicting parts of these animals on their religious paraphernalia.

Still Viable as a Religion

If Shamanism was mankind's earliest religion, it has largely disappeared in most areas when they become industrialized. Korea is an exception. Although presently one of the leaders among the world's rapidly developing countries, Shamanism still flourishes as a religion in south Korea, even influencing other faiths such as Buddhism and Christianity. A recent survey reported that one in every 380 Koreans has had some

This Shang-dynasty bronze vessel (c.1200 B.C.) would have held sacrificial offerings. Within the intricate scrollwork, fanciful animal designs can be seen.

A *tol harubang,* or stone grandfather from Korea's Cheju Island. The origin of these shamanistic statues is uncertain, but they most probably reflect an Oceanic origin.

A ceremony of *Hanul Kyo* or "The Religion of Heaven," a modern revival of a sect of Korea's traditional faith, with Tangun, Korea's legendary founder, as its chief deity. Taken at Mari-san in May, 1980.

psychic experience in his or her lifetime. Over 70,000 spirit-mediums are dues-paying members of a Mudang Association in Seoul. To understand much of Korea's cultural background, a knowledge of Shamanistic practices, both of the past and the present, is really a necessity.

A Complex Heritage

Not only is Shamanism very much alive in Korea, it has survived through the centuries in spite of persecution by Buddhists, Neo-Confucianists and lately by Christians, and people of no religion. Furthermore, Korea has not one type of Shamanism today, but many. The rituals differ from province to province, almost as various denominations of Protestant churches may have quite divergent services.

Somewhat as Christianity can be divided into two basic branches (Catholic and Pro-

One of the "northern style" dolmens, this is on Kanghwa Island near Inchon. Even at this early period, the differentiations between northern and southern styles of Shamanism were evident, for the "southern style" dolmens were built much closer to the ground.

testant), so Korea's Shamanism can be divided into two basic types, namely the northern branch in which the medium is "called" by the spirit and ecstasy became an integral part of the rituals and a second type, generally termed "southern branch" in which the profession is hereditary and ecstasy is rarely involved.

The southern type appears to flourish in a large segment of south Korea today. One variant can be witnessed on Cheju Island. In the southwestern part of the peninsula, the Cholla provinces have a somewhat different type, while the east coast also has its distinctive rituals. Spirit intermediaries of the southern type pass on their knowledge of propitious chants and rituals in a hereditary fashion, either through the daughter-in-law or the daughter. They operate in a limited area, almost becoming a parish priest, and receive an annual fee for calendar-related performances. If special, personalized service is needed, this requires additional money.

In the Seoul area and extending down the peninsula's center to Taegu, a different type of Shamanism is practiced. This branch once flourished in what is now north Korea. Professional ability does NOT descend through the family line. Rather the spirits summon a young person to become an intermediary, using "shaman sickness" or *shinbyong* lasting from days to years intermittently. Its only cure is to become a medium, at which time an experienced teacher must be found.

This branch of Shamanism is more closely linked to practices and symbolism which flourished on the Siberian Steppes until Communism suppressed it. Its historic background suggests the wild horseback nomads. Its art reflects the white birch tree which in cold climates became an important symbol. Possession by the spirits is an everyday occurrence with these mediums. They are called *manshin* meaning literally "ten thousand spirits" and in theory are capable of summoning or being possessed by an infinite number. The males are called *paksu*.

Agricultural Shamanism or Musok

The earliest literary record of shaman activity in the Far East is a series of songs or chants sung during the Chou dynasty (1123-256 B.C.) in China. The shamaness performed for the court in China with agricultural rituals until the Han dynasty substituted Confucian ceremonies. Prehistoric rites for a good harvest or the blessings of the ancestors were performed by *wu* in China, who seem to bear some relation to the *mu* of Korea, where they are still known by the general term of *mudang*. Folklorists at some of Korea's universities are busy recording the narrative songs or *muga*, sung by the mudang who practice in south Korea. These songs form a sort of oral reservoir of myth and legend going back about two millennia.

Less than a century ago King Kojong was offering sacrifices to the Earth Spirit to insure a good harvest for the farmers.

This mural from the "Tomb of the Dancers," reflects the horseback life of the peoples of Koguryo. Before the arrival of Buddhist influence, Shamanist beliefs were that the afterlife was the same as normal life, thus the hunters in the tomb can be seen pursuing deer, even though they fly over mountaintops in a spiritual context.

A bronze belt buckle and clasp, with a horse and sunburst design, showing the northern Shamanistic talismans of greatest importance, the sun and the horse.

21

Manshin at an altar

Shinto shrine at Pyongyang during colonial period.

Queen Min was patronizing a mudang to intercede with the Birth Grandmother and bless her with a son to succeed to the throne. Throughout the country, Shamanism was the basic folk faith of the largely agricultural nation. Droughts could be cured by sufficient prayers to the Rain Dragon.

When the Japanese took control of Korea, they attacked *musok* (the folk religion) as mere superstition, but this suppression was also aimed at destroying Korea's ancient cultural roots. The colonial powers sought to substitute their own branch of Shamanism, which had been changed into Shintoism with a heavy admixture of emperor-worship. A Shinto shrine the Japanese built in Pyongyang is illustrated here. However, in secret the mudangs taught the songs to their heirs and the fishermen on Cheju Island supported their own mediator with the Dragon King of the Sea to insure a good catch or a safe return. As long as Korea remained basically a non-industrialized nation, the Mountain Spirit would have his followers and the Roof Beam Spirit be paid his due.

Industrialization succeeded better than the Japanese had in suppressing rites to the multiple spirits. The nuclear family, apartment house living, subways, trains and airplanes rather eliminated the world of spirits.

Only just as Korea was about to lose her ancient heritage, the lesson of what had happened in China and Japan became apparent to leaders of present-day Korea. The new Ministry of Culture woke up.

Seoul's Urban Shamanism Based on Hunting Traditions of Long Ago

The manshin's power during a kut rests primarily on ability to become possessed by one or more spirits in succession, to throw herself into a trance of rapture and travel vast distances, riding on the beat of a drum. This ability is precipitated by a group who need assistance because they or some relative is sick. But the manshin themselves have gone through a spiritual sickness, with visions, hallucinations and various unusual behavior which is part of the spirit's "calling" and is cured only through initiation by a mature shaman. Then the new spirit-medium begins a career of magical practices to serve these troubled individuals, families or sections of a community.

The bells in the performer's hand, the costumes, the portraits—all descend from very ancient times when Korea was first populated by a race of hunters, and then gradually accommodated itself to an agricultural tradition. Movements, paraphernalia and artistic props—these present a kaleidoscope of the history of the Korean people, their hopes and fears, their beliefs down through the ages, from prehistory to the present.

Communist Suppression

In 1948 when he took over the dictatorship of North Korea, Kim Il-sung tried to eliminate all religions (except Marxist-Leninist-Kimism and some puppet Buddhism for propaganda). By 1970 organized religions had been largely abolished north of the truce line.

Meanwhile, during the Korean War from 1950 to 1953, those shamans of the northern or ecstatic tradition who were then young as well as prosperous enough to travel, or lived close to the border to make the trip feasible, "voted with their feet," taking advantage of wartime's confusion.

It has been estimated that at least several million North Koreans came south or "crossed over to freedom." Of this multitude, an unknown number, but surely hundreds of manshin of the ecstatic type

managed to reach Seoul. Some of them are now dead but the younger ones are still alive and have disciples.

The Star of the Show

During the summer of 1982, for the celebration of the Korean-American Centennial, two dozen performers, representing all the main provinces (mostly from outside of Seoul), were flown in to dance at the Mall in Washington D.C., as well as at Knoxville's World's Fair. Also these practitioners of the folk faith type of singing and dancing helped inaugurate a folk painting exhibit at Los Angeles County's Craft and Folk Art Museum, which showed Zo Zayong's tiger paintings, now at his private Emileh Museum at Songni-san.

In every city, the millions who attended appreciated one dancer the most; she was the acknowledged star. Interestingly, this stellar shaman dancer is among those who fled south during the Korean War. Called by the spirit world at eleven to become a manshin, she was in her twenties when the Korean War came. Now in her early fifties,

Kim Kum-hwa, performing a ritual for more than 200 onlookers at Samgak Mountain, on the eve of the June full moon in 1982.

23

Closeup of Kim Kum-hwa in a later stage of the same section of the literary spirit ritual, wielding a brass knife.

Kim Kum-hwa is the acknowledged leader in the tradition of northern-type ecstatic Shamanism, which once dominated north Korea and is still prevalent in the Seoul area, though not in the southern provinces. She has disciples, including the first American citizen initiated into this difficult profession.

Attractions of Northern Shamanism

Ecstatic dances are more dramatic than the lengthy chants or songs of southern mudang when one is unfamiliar with the words. Northern Shamanism seems to involve more brilliant colors in its costumes and a more insistent beat in its music. The dancing is vigorous to the point of being feverish and the plot or cast of characters appears to be more involved in the present than dependent on historical references in an archaic language, difficult for any except a few folklore scholars. Northern Shaman-

A manshin possessed by a general.

ism touches the restless cord found in

Performance by a male shaman on Mt. Samgak in June, 1982.

people dwelling in northern temperate and subarctic climates, to whom nature has been both a friend and enemy, its myriad creations a source of both wonder and danger. For those who do not believe in the world of spirits, it is still good theater! For those who are open-minded, it will raise a few doubts.

For the art historian, the northern or Siberian type of ritual holds interest because its group of icons or portraits of favorite deities presents visual challenges. These icons furnish psychological support to the shaman, especially at the beginning and finale of a ceremony. They also help the viewer understand the development of Korean cultural expression.

Anthropologists may note similarities between present-day ecstatic rituals or paraphernalia and those which early nineteenth-century Russian scholars recorded as being used in Siberia and the Altai Mountains.

Shamanism was being practiced there and still is to some degree, as the present-day Communists no longer actively persecute folk religions of the minorities.

Archeologists can relate Siberia's visual symbolism to the artifacts uncovered in Silla's fifth and sixth-century tombs, or even earlier objects recently excavated in the Kaya States' region. Indeed, fascinating speculations arise when one compares visual similarities between present-day shaman accouterments and many thousands of artifacts uncovered from Korea's ancient tombs. Ritual objects created fifteen centuries ago were designed at a time when Siberian-type Shamanism commanded loyalty in the Silla Kingdom, involving the wealth of its gold mines. Although Korean Shamanism has very little written history in comparison with Buddhism, through archeology and art history one can leap back a millennium and a half in imagination and thus visualize Korean Shamanism of the northern type in its period of greatest glory.

Fresco in North Korea.

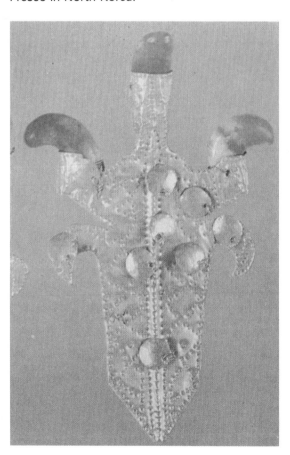

2 CHARISMATIC SHAMAN SYMBOLS OF THE PAST AND PRESENT

The golden jewelry unearthed in recent decades from Kyongju's mounded tombs always excites and amazes viewers. During the "5,000 Years of Korean Art Exhibit," held in the United States for two years at eight museums or touring European Museum in 1984 the intricately fabricated golden crowns aroused tremendous wonderment. These golden objects were not created in a cultural vacuum, but designed to fit in with a certain context of life as it was happening fifteen hundred years ago on the southeastern part of the Korean peninsula. At that time Shamanism with Siberian antecedents was the Korean state religion. It held in thrall the riches of the realm, including the output of Silla's gold mines.

Accessory for a beaten gold crown of the Kaya kingdom representing a magical deer with an extra horn in the center of its forehead. This "central horn" indication of magic power can be seen in 17th century Korean ink painting as well. Hoam Museum, Yongin Family Land.

Shaman-kings held a charismatic royal power so that multitudes of artisans created burial objects for them. These artifacts suggest ancient Shamanistic beliefs of great potency in this long ago vanished world. These symbols cry out to be interpreted.

Dr. Li Ogg is Korea's foremost scholar in this field. He heads the Center of Korean Studies at the College de France. Li has suggested that many of the objects in Kyong-ju's golden horde "have connections with the nomads of the northern steppes." This book follows his lead; it seeks to examine more closely the clues which language and archeology offer to connect fifth-century Silla with its antecedents.

Linguistic scholars normally classify the Korean language as part of an Altai group of languages, a vast family which stretches from Finland, Hungary and Turkey to Korea. In like manner, archeology seems to indicate a group of Shamanistic symbols or a family of artistic motifs which once ruled the Siberian Steppes and traveled south-ward to Korea, some of them being taken to Japan by its Korean conquerors.

On the northern border of Mongolia, in the Altai Mountains region, excavations

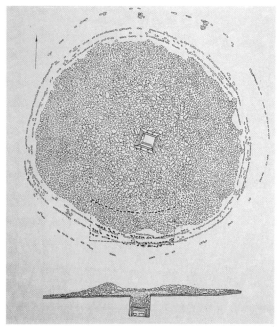

A line drawing of an Altai tomb in Siberia. The basic structure is the same as that found in Kyongju. Earlier, similar examples still dot the northern fastness in a line from Korea towards the heart of Siberia.

Tumuli Park in Kyongju, in the Kyongsang province of Korea. At times the larger mounds, with more ornate burial objects are those of women, not men. (5-6c. A.D.)

A carpet from a Mongolian Altai tomb, showing a Persian-style griffin attacking a Siberian elk. (first century A.D.)

have uncovered numerous burial mounds not unlike Kyongju's in shape and size. Silla's tallest mound is 75 feet (23 meters) while the tallest Altai mound is 69 feet (21 meters). Such rounded mounds in the Altai region belonged to those shaman-chieftains who once roamed a steppe trail then without a name, one further north than the Silk Road, which became so famous later on.

These Altai tombs extend over a half millennium for the dates of their erection. Usually the tombs were attacked by grave robbers, who carried away the metal objects, probably melting them down for their component gold. The coffins were buried beneath the region's permafrost level, in pits three to six meters under the earth. After the grave robbers ransacked a tomb, they frequently failed to seal it properly; thus the surrounding ground water seeped in and froze the remaining burial objects into solid blocks of ice. Materials more fragile than metal, such as leather, felt and fur have been perfectly preserved because of such

climatic conditions. Over 5,000 objects have been removed from Altai tombs.

Normally perishable items such as embroidered silk textiles, knotted rugs or felt appliques (sealed into the permafrost), have been recovered in near-perfect condition for twentieth-century archeologists to ponder. Because the Altai herdsman practiced a northern type of Shamanism, these objects offer some light on the mythos of fifth-century Silla burial objects.

The horse and the deer seem to be important symbols in these Altai shaman burials. Religious beliefs evidently were based on a unity of the human and animal world. Hunting was partly for food, but also served as a ritual activity. In one Altaic *kurgan* (tomb) excavated first by two Russians in 1929 and later thoroughly researched by the famous Rudenko in 1947 and 1949, a number of artifacts recall the Silla tombs.

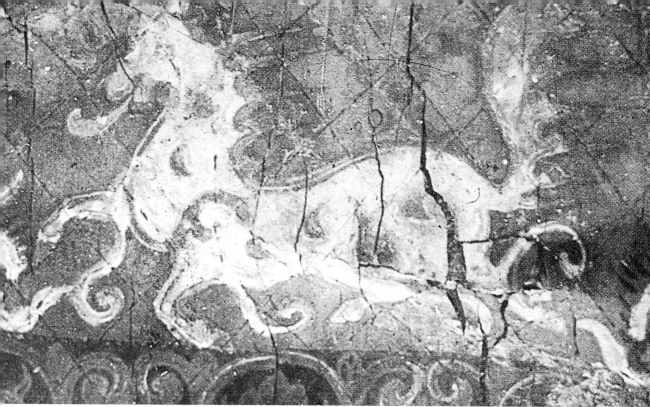

Birchbark painting of a "Heavenly Horse," from the Heavenly Horse Tomb of ancient Silla. The suggestion of four "extra legs gives the magic horse its ability to fly.

Horses in Ancient Shaman Rituals

In 1973, while excavating Tomb #155 at Kyongju, the Koreans discovered ritualistic horse paintings *on birchbark* made upon saddle flaps. Silla's shaman-kings had been buried with horses and horse trappings so Tomb #155 was renamed "Heavenly Horse Tomb" because of these paintings on birchbark. Most old Altai tombs included horses buried in numbers. Pazyryk V, dated about 300 B.C., contained the bodies of ten richly-caprisoned horses (See drawing). These horses lead the procession of the shaman-ruler to heaven. The lead animals were lavishly decorated with saddles and bridles, motifs worked out in gold and tin, but also relief designs *in birchbark*. (The white birch was the sacred tree of the shamans across the Steppes area, and its sacredness was carried to Silla.)

This particular mound contained not only ten horses, but the bodies of a Mongoloid ruler and his Europoid wife. The

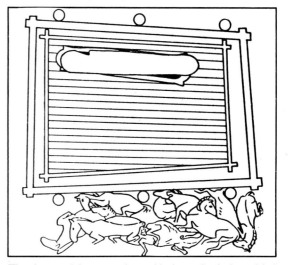

The internal layout of an Altai tomb dating third century B.C. Ten horses were placed next to the burial chamber to accompany the ruler to his kingdom in the afterlife. The sarcophagus was at the extreme wall of the wooden chamber constructed as a vault in the mound.

symbolism of the horses' decoration featured reindeer (See drawing), also important in Silla's Shamanistic art. The leather-garmented horses included one with a mask suggesting a reindeer and others with horse-like appearances except for two "wings" with pseudo-feathers of carved leather. This suggests that the winged horse would lead the procession to the afterlife by virtue of his power of flight. (This recalls the wings in the crown of the Heavenly Horse Tomb of Kyongju, suggesting flight to heaven.)

Mircea Eliade in his book, *Shamanism: Archaic Techniques of Ecstasy* tells of the sacrificial horse being killed in a cruel way by breaking its spine. The soul of the horse would then fly off to heaven, bearing the prayers of the shaman and his wishes for an audience with the gods.

The inhabitants of Silla do not seem to have been so cruel, being more removed from nomadic life. An earthenware vessel survives in the shape of a horse and rider from a Silla tomb which has been labeled "a ceremonial drinking vessel." However, what particular ceremony would require a vessel designed like this? (see this page) The horse itself is hollow, with a drinking spout coming from the animal's chest. In Mithraism a priest was consecrated by being given a literal "bath" in the blood of an ox. This would be done by having the priest step into a pit, covering it, then having an ox stand over it. The breast of the bull would then be pierced with a sword or spear, the heart blood of the bull rushing out to baptize the priest.

The Buryat of Siberia would hold a goat over a shaman's head and do the same thing, although the Buryat sometimes drank the blood as well. Could this Kyongju vessel in the form of a horse with a spout in its chest have been used to catch the horse's blood during a ritual as it poured

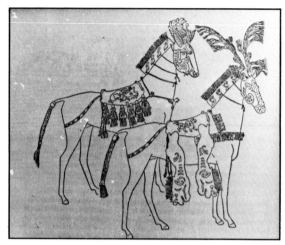

Two "lead horses" from the tomb of a Siberian Altai ruler. One horse bears leather reindeer horns, while the other wears a cap with leather wings, to lift the ruler's chariot train to the upper levels of heaven in the afterlife.

A horse and rider ceramic vessel. Some mystery exists on the exact nature of this vessel. By following rituals which extend from fourth century B.C. Scythia, through Mithraism to nineteenth century Buryat initiations, this vessel was for drinking blood pumped from the horse's still living heart. Seoul National Museum.

forth? Then the shaman-king of Silla could drink the blood from the spout, thus symbolically drinking the horse's heart blood. This would explain the location of the drinking spout on this earthenware vessel, as well as the vessel's peculiar shape.

Flight to Heaven Symbolism

The Siberian shaman's ability to fly to heaven to commune with spirits was a very major part of his powers. Most of the Kyongju golden crowns have two wings attached to the headbands or the inner crown. Furthermore, most shamans performing in Korea today have some sort of bird feathers attached to their hats.

A three-legged bird has religious symbolism connected with the south and the sun; Korea seems to have derived this from China. But the concept of the "flying horse" suggests a northern derivation.

The basic concept of unity between the world of humans and the world of animals, including birds, is born out by this symbolism. Levitation or "flight" has been a valued prerogative of those entering into altered states of consciousness in many areas long before the airplane was invented.

The symbolic power to fly to heaven was incorporated into the golden crowns of Silla, since most of the crowns are dominated by two golden wings, decorated with round sun symbols. The *Wei-chih* mentioned that the people of Chin-Han, (an older name for Silla) were buried with bird wings to assist them in heavenward flight.

Several Koguryo tombs have people mounted on fantastic animals, all with the power of flight. The goose is included as he was often the vehicle for the Altai shaman to fly to heaven.

One particular crown from the "Heavenly Horse Tomb" (*Chonmachong*) has the clearest amount of symbolism which sug-

Gold horse mask from the Heavenly Horse Tomb, Kyongju. Wearing this in the crown would give the shaman-ruler the power of flight and the strength of a horse.

gests a connection with the horse rituals of the Altais still performed in the nineteenth century according to Eliade. The crown itself has a "horse mask" which fits into a place in the top of the crown. This would signify that the shaman-ruler could borrow the power of the horse in his divinations. By using all of this varied animal symbolism, the shaman practitioner would acquire the strength, speed, endurance and power of all the animals represented.

The most convincing evidence to suggest that the "Heavenly Horse" of Tomb #155 is indeed the shaman's magic horse is the painting mentioned before and illustrated on page 29.

The "Heavenly Horse" of the Buryat tribal shamans in Siberia is reported to have "eight legs." The extra four are those that give it the special power of flight. Korea's "Heavenly Horse" painted on the birch

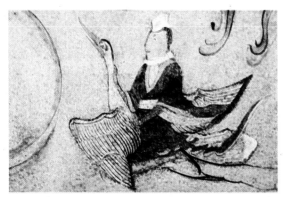

A shaman on a heavenward flight upon the back of a goose. From a sixth-century Koguryo tomb mural.

Koguryo bronze openwork showing the three-legged crow of the sun, a later Chinese strain introduced into Korean Shamanism. Pyongyang Museum.

Later Koguryo tomb mural showing Chinese Taoist influence with a very Confucian king riding a dragon, followed by a shaman on a multi-colored flying horse.

Koguryo tomb mural showing several types of flying fantastic animals. One section shows a flying horse with well-developed tufts of hair at its ankles, which if extended would equal the "magic eight legs" of the Heavenly Horse of Silla.

bark saddle flap seems to be equipped with "eight legs," the extra four being somewhat different.

In the color plate, the Heavenly Horse seems to be puffing with might and main, tongue hanging out, and striding upwards through clouds. The four "extra legs" do not seem quite like legs, but it is the symbolism which is important, not the actuality or realism of representation. Koguryo tomb paintings show tufts of hair, but the Silla painting on birch bark shows more fanciful "tufts" which have turned into legs, to support the magical flight.

The uplifted tail of this horse in Tomb #155 seems to indicate some Arabian blood in his veins, as opposed to the short, stocky Mongolian pony type. The "flying tail" is consistent as a trait with Arab horses. This possibly represents a special breed kept for the use of royalty, as was the case with Altai shaman-chieftain centuries before.

The "final flight" at death was the most important one, of course, but the practicing shaman often flew (as a spirit, of course) in

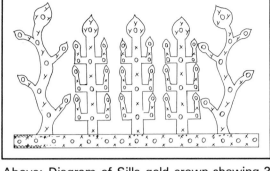

Above: Diagram of Silla gold crown showing 3 cosmic trees and 2 deer antlers. N.T. #87.

Left: Sketch of crown at Novocherkask, South U.S.S.R., first century B.C. Scythian.

search of a soul which had left its body due to the action of malign spirits. Or the shaman might fly on the back of a goose to the abode of the heavenly king.

The modern Siberian shaman's headdress is decorated with feathers to indicate his mastery of the air. Ability to fly or seeming to fly was a necessary part of the divination rituals which were practiced.

Stag Antlers (Siberian Reindeer) in Shaman Ritual

The presence of antlers fabricated from gold on most of the major crowns unearthed in Kyongju would seem to be another link to the nomads of the northern steppes, where reverence for the reindeer, especially the stag and his antlers, was universal.

The Altai not only used the reindeer as a chief source of food, but they nominated him as a constellation and a magic animal. Ceremonies grew up around this creature's most notable feature, the antlers. Reindeer became associated with the movement of the sun through the sky. One legend records that a reindeer held the sun between his antlers. Or a deer with golden antlers was responsible for the east-to-west movement of the sun across Siberia each day.

The fact that the reindeer was believed to have been a celestial animal made his antlers into powerful talismans, by associative magic and thus their use on the ruler's crowns in Silla-period tombs. It is reported that in Siberia ancient shamans who wished to call back deer herds, which had vanished in a blizzard or been dispersed by a pack of wolves, would wear upon their heads reindeer antlers made of natural horn or fabricated from iron. Thus they hoped to be able to converse with the spirit of the animals and through sympathetic magic force the herd to return.

One Siberian legend construes the heavenly elk as the cause of solar eclipses; he carries the sun into the underworld with his antlers. Probably the shaman on the Steppes had a special ceremony for dealing with this frightening phenomena. As recently as a hundred years ago, the costumes of Siberian shamans in the areas where reindeer formed the mainstay of life, included a magic cap with antlers represented in iron.

Silla gold crown, clearly showing prominent stag antlers.

Above: Prince or princess' crown, showing the three levels of heaven which the wearer could travel by the number of branches on the Cosmic Tree, National Museum.
Right: A full-sized Silla crown, with seven branches on the Cosmic Tree, indicating the wearer could travel through seven levels of heaven. National Museum.

Perhaps the middle-aged or elderly Korean wife who pays $1,000 for an ounce of shavings which have come from the velvet of deer horn, does not realize that the power of the deer has ancient roots when she visits the herbal medicine shop. Virility and longevity became associated with deer antlers in the mists of antiquity.

Altai tombs have revealed countless objects pointing to the deer as a sacred symbol, whether fabricated in gold, wood, leather or bone. Descendants of these mounted rulers of the Altai, when they moved eastward, spread both their language and their religious symbols far and wide. Almost equally important in the structure of their sacred symbols, besides the reindeer and his antlers, was the white birch, Siberia's holy tree.

Cosmic Tree (The White Birch), Center of the Cosmos

Every crown discovered at Kyongju displays tree-shaped ornaments rising from its headband. Normally three such forms stand upright. These stylized trees, with branches jutting off at right angles, resent the World Tree or the Cosmic Tree, which was a major symbol across the whole northern Siberian Steppes. In nature one species, both very beautiful and unusual, the white birch, became a special symbol for Shamanism. Today very few white birch grow in south Korea, but further north where the winters are much more severe the birch is common. It grows in a northern latitude all the way across Eurasia from Finland and the Scandinavian countries to northern Korea.

The birch and its special significance to northern-type Shamanism may be very ancient. Professor Li Ogg of the University of Paris has pointed out that the first component of the name "Tangun," Korea's traditional founder, is "tan" signifying a variety of birch. According to the ancient story, Tan'gun was born under a birch tree on the slopes of Whitehead Mountain, on the border between Manchuria and present-day North Korea. Such a cold climate would produce many white birch.

· Although the concept of a Cosmic Tree seems universal among Siberian tribes, it is more difficult to trace this symbol back to the Altai tombs. In the same mound or kurgan that revealed the procession of ten horses, a tapestry was found representing a ruler of Mongoloid appearance holding a stylized tree in his hand, seated upon a throne while receiving a Europoid visitor on horseback. (This same ruler had a Europoid wife and perhaps the majority of the population was not Mongoloid. The Altai maintained a highly mobile society, exchanging gifts as far away as China.)

The tapestry shows a tree held in the ruler's hand, a symbol which seems like a scepter. Perhaps this indicates the ceremonial importance in rituals using a tree as a symbol of royalty.

In *Shamanism: Archaic Techniques of Ecstasy*, Eliade discusses tree symbolism at great length. The Yakut shamans on the western border of the Altai Mountains as well as the Buryat, located to the north, both retained the ritual symbolism of climbing a tree for the shaman to reach heaven.

The Cosmic Tree in itself represents the central pillar of the universe in Siberian Shamanism. Its roots are planted in the underworld, its trunk in the world of man and its branches in heaven, so the shaman may visit all three realms. This would ex-

An early (3rd-4th century A.D.) Kaya crown, made of gilt bronze. Coarser construction indicates this may have been a battle crown, with three levels of heaven represented. Kyemyong University Museum, Taegu.

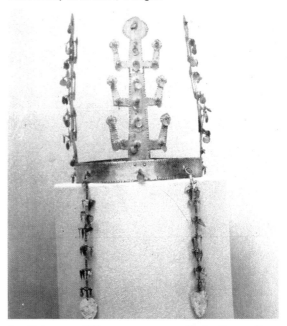

A gilt bronze Silla crown presently in the collection of the Ho-am Museum. The Cosmic Tree is the central feature of this work, indicating perhaps that the single most important symbol in ancient Silla's Shamanism was the Cosmic Tree.

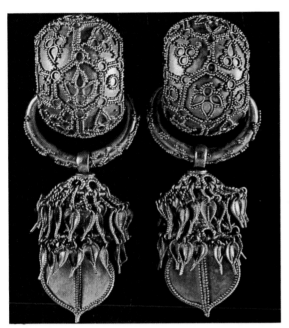

Birch-leaf shaped earrings, found in Silla tombs. Many diverse types of these earrings were discovered, but all have the palmate shape of two different species of birch sacred to Siberian Shamanism.

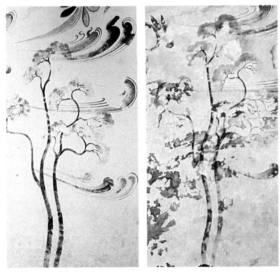

A Koguryo tomb mural showing birch trees thrusting skyward through the wind, Trees of this sort are a common denominator of Koguryo tombs from the fifth and sixth centuries.

plain why all the crowns of Silla's shaman-kings display tree designs rising from the circlet, which was itself decorated with waves to represent the ocean or the under world.

On the golden crowns unearthed from Kyongju's burial mounds, the number of branches varies slightly. Most have seven ends, three on each side and the top end branch, although two crowns among those so far discovered have nine. This may be explained if the number of branches refers to the levels of heaven. Some tribes had seven and others had nine levels of heaven in their mythology. The uppermost branch became the residence of the chief deity.

Jewelry as Golden Birch Leaves

A Shamanist tale survives about a "Goddess of the Tree of Life." She sits amongst the branches of the Cosmic Tree, controlling the fate of men. This magical tree has a million leaves, with each man's fate written upon one leaf. When the goddess causes a particular leaf to fall, that human being dies.

The jewelry excavated from Kyongju evidences two shapes, both of which are similar to the shape of a birch leaf in real life (See crown page 33). The long pendants with so many golden leaf shapes clinging to their strands suggest a reflection of the power of the shaman-king over the multitudinous lives of his subjects. Earrings also often have birth-leaf shapes as their decoration.

This jewelry suggests a belief that the shaman-ruler controlled the life and death of his subjects, as, indeed, he did. During the fifth century Shamanism was the state religion of the Silla Kingdom; it was merely the accepted thing that the king, who was the highest shaman in the kingdom, also took the lion's share of the treasures available, thus ensuring the blessings of the spirits.

Bones as Shaman Magic

Another factor which ties the beliefs of Siberian Shamanists with the aristocrats of ancient Silla in the fifth and sixth century, one which seems to have lingered on, is the significance of "bones" as magic or semi-magic. In Silla a gradation of its nobility was known as "bone ranks." The level of a person in the noble class was determined by his parents' stature. In the West this might be considered a bloodline, but Siberian Shamanism conceived it as linked to the nature of the body's bones; they were the determinant factor for a person's status in life.

In his initiation dream, a Siberian shaman-priest would see himself "scraped down to his bones," which were then treated by his tutelary spirit, so as to survive the rigors of this religion and also life on earth as a shaman or spirit-medium.

People in modern Siberia are still called "the descendant of so and so's bone." Lineage was conceived as related to "bone" in the social position of the Silla rulers, they were chosen from the "holy bone" group. They were allowed to govern the country as its religious-temporal rulers, while the "true bone" people made up the noble class. Those without "bone rank" were the lower classes.

In the societies of both the Altai and the people of Silla, the power of one's bones provided protection against evil forces. (This might be because a fracture in primitive times would lead to a lingering death in most cases.) Thus the significance of "bones" and their effect on a person's well being, or his ability to repel evil spirits, can be associated with the condition of an individual's bones. Certain objects on the Silla rulers belts may be an abstract design of "bones" rendered into golden jewelry. (This is the author's idea, not yet confirmed by other art historians.)

Historical Speculations

Archeology presents intriguing parallels between the Altai tombs and those of fifth-century Silla, both so full of horses as significant symbols of their Shamanistic religions. yet how to account for the distance in time and space? One Chinese record, titled the *Wei-chih*, dated in the early third century A.D., describes the travels of Chinese who went from their own Wei kingdom to study the land they said was inhabited by "Eastern Barbarians." These records fail to indicate a society based on hunting, in which horses were a major cultural factor.

Is it possible that the inhabitants of southeastern Korea were different then? The *Samguk Yusa* written by a Buddhist monk in 1145 A.D. gives apocryphal accounts concerning the genesis of the three kingdoms of Korea. A group called "Eastern Puyo" were told to leave the area of their habitation (in Manchuria) and move to the east. They seem to disappear in the East Sea in the early third century A.D. This would have put them in Silla if they moved in a southeasterly direction. The *Wei-chih* mentioned previously, describes the Eastern Puyo as among the most civilized of those the Chinese thought of as "barbarians." The Puyo were makers of fine white cloth as well as breeders of superb horses.

The group in a position to make the Eastern Puyo move southward out of Manchuria was the rising kingdom of Koguryo. It is known to have battled with a Chinese army from the Wei kingdom in 243 A.D., in the area formerly adjacent to the Puyo who had gone south and east. A history of Korea written over a hundred years ago by a professor at Tokyo University, who may have had access to records now lost, attributes the southward movement of the Puyo to the real founding of large scale king-

A line drawing of Ko Chumong, the legendary founder of Koguryo, crossing the Sungari Reiver on the backs of turtles and fish.

"Flying Horse Tomb" in Japan. This tomb in Kyushu has a Heavenly Horse at the top of the painting, but at the base a horse can be seen being unloaded from a boat by a human in Continental dress.

doms in the Korean peninsula. According to that book, the Puyo were much more advanced than the smaller, tribal groups they overcame. They were semi-nomadic with a culture quite dependent on horses.

Further archeological excavations may offer more definitive answers to this puzzling question. But it is known that the Altai were Shamanistic, the Puyo had shaman-kings, Silla had shaman-kings and a group of Puyo put their horses on boats and invaded Japan in 369 A.D., bringing to it a culture of rounded burial mounds and the horse as a major figure. In fact, they are termed "The Horseriders." They bestowed their brand of Shamanism upon Japan where it is still known as "The Way of the Spirits" or *Shin-to*. Superior technology and a system of cavalry enabled the Puyo to unify Japan, then divided into many agricultural communities. Perhaps it is not too surprising that the Japanese language is classified by linguists as "in the Altai family."

The bird in the boat, a Japanese tumuli painting signifying the true landing place of the Puyo noble who later became Japan's first emperor.

3 PATHS TO ALTERNATE REALITIES

Music: First Steps upon the Path

"Music hath charms. . ." the saying goes. Over the centuries music has been used to stir human hearts into a stronger effort, or to unite them in common cause, such as martial music sending millions to their deaths with internal inspiration. "Working songs" have been used to release people from the drudgery of tasks, to divorce workers from the unpleasant and difficult jobs facing them. Of all the types of music that are used with a definite purpose in mind, perhaps none has a more powerful effect than music used for religious reasons; it stirs devotion to a holy cause, or more graphically outlines the tortures which await the deviant "sinner" in the particular hell propagated by that faith.

Music, when used in ecstatic shaman rituals actually does none of the above; it is the first step to divorce the medium from the mundane or secular world, to allow the mind of the medium to commune with or be possessed by spirits. The basic music in Korean Shamanism is that which could have been made by the most primitive men, that of the rhythmic beat of a drum, whose insistent deep tones disrupt the natural flow of the body's rhythm, speeding or slowing it, causing the mind of the audience and participants to open upon a different reality.

The next most important instruments in Korean Shamanist rituals are meals "gongs" or cymbals, the kind which first came into being in the Bronze Age, when a metal-smith was a type of shaman, for did he not take special types of rocks, then transmute them into useful implements? These basic instruments are the ones always seen at kuts, those classified as "percussion," whose striking, discordant manipulations could stir frenzy or create peace.

A *manshin* in trance, twirling in a circle, to the accompaniment of the hourglass drum and small gong.

Painting from Sungjon University Museum showing a performing shaman and the two basic accompanying instruments.

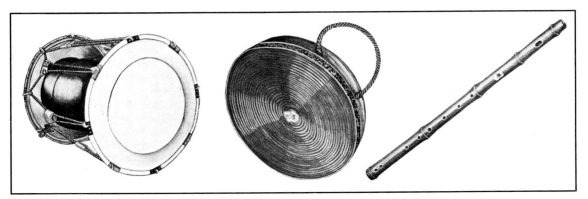

Line drawing of the basic musical instruments used in a kut.

A mudang's brass wand which contains from five to nine jingle bells. These are considered to have magic power. This *kal* (knife) would be used to drive out demons.

The music at Korean Shamanist rituals allows the manshin to divorce herself from the mundane, such as taxes and family squabbles; she is allowed to meet the spirits with an empty and pure mind, to become a suitable vessel to pass along commands and advice from the world which is real but unseen to those who deal in the profane.

Bells, Spears and Knives

Three metal accessories rank among the most important and necessary of the spirit-medium's; they are always used during the dance. These sacred objects may go back to the Bronze Age, when Shamanism was Korea's only religion. A group of brass bells, which look like the jangling accoutrements seen in modern parades, may represent precisely that, horse bells, used to summon or repel spirits. These bells are given a brass handle or a cloth strap, and will be shaken at times during the ritual, particularly when the spirits are most needed. The manshin might also wave this wand in a sort of blessing, rubbing it in the fat which exudes from the meat offering, thereby extending blessing when casting it out over the crowd in attendance.

A long-handled spear, called a *chang,* in the shape of a trident (similar to Neptune's trident), is sometimes seen in the hands of the more aggressive spirits when their portraits are tendered. A crescent-moon shaped halberd, excellent for slicing through the breast-bone of an enemy is also seen; this is called a *kom.* Used in exorcism rituals by any of the generals or overseer spirits, it can have both long or short handles. Being shapened cold iron, it is one of the most useful demon-terrifying instruments, a sign of supreme martial and magic potency.

Manshin as ancestral spirit.

Ritual Dancing

The movements of the dance which accompany the kut indeed have a semi-prescribed pattern. Although certain basic steps are followed, when the manshin is in trance, in possession, she moves as the spirits direct her, in what the non-initiate might call an "ad lib." This is not the case in a real sense, for the shaman moves as the spirits direct her; her movements reflect their movements, their ecstasy, spirit borne, whether as the majestic, heavenly and measured steps of the literary spirits, or the frenzied dance of the general-spirit in the midst of combat, he who senses the death of his mortal enemy, or subjugation of a proud prince, whether demonic or historical.

Some of the dances by the female shamans are sensuous and somewhat ribald. When tempting the wandering spirit into the spirit house which resembles a coffin, they rub the spirit house on the lower parts of their bodies, in a sort of tempting manner. The spirit house is to take those souls which do not wish to leave the earthly plane and firmly escort them to the underworld. The shaman will accompany them on this trip, delivering the errant spirit to its pre-deceased family members, showing it the not-so-radically-different world of the afterlife, which the wandering spirit had previously avoided.

Present-day Shamanist performances, those seen at Seoul's National Theatre or in what might be termed a "civilized" environment, have all the theatre aspects that one can find at a shaman ritual, but lack the insistent movement of a kut which is given for a client who believes in the power of the spirits. To see a somewhat frail sixty-year old woman begin to strike a client when in the persona of a general (The client was apparently trying to economize on the money offering to the general whose presence he had requested.), then be a normal, slightly chatty woman after the end of the "seance," indicates just how far into possession some manshin are while in trance, and how real the occupying presence is, for the dance in this case should have dislocated her neck.

Musicians and Their Instruments

The hourglass drum is seen at every kut. The musician's left palm is used to strike the left side of this drum (*changgo*), with the right side hit by a wooden rod. A small gong of brass (*ching*), is also used to summon the spirits to attend.

A large-sized, circular drum is hit by both men and women, but more by men. It is made of wood with cow's hide stretched across both sides. A more delicate musical effect is reached by the use of a gourd. This is floated in a jar of water and then lightly tapped with the fingertips while floating. Occasionally a cup-shaped brass bell is beaten with a piece of deer horn; this is called "the bell of the princess." It is decorated with silken streamers.

A special mood is added when flutes are played, the larger size being about two feet in length. A reed instrument is sometimes used when the spirit-medium is calling for the spirit of the dead to appear. It has an eerie sound. Metal mirrors also may be included, being shaken as the spirit-medium dances. Mirrors are round or square, and seem to refer to very ancient sun worship.

Although a manshin controls the kut, dances and chants and summons the ten thousand spirits, she needs a minimum of two musicians (male or female or both) and one woman assistant to help with the changes of clothing, to light cigarettes, hand her a sword or a cup of cloudy rice wine (*makkoli*), switch fans, hold a bucket or whatever other stage business needs doing.

Some really good musicians become so involved in the repetitive beat of their own

Manshin as martial spirit, with her musician-assistants, who will also help her change clothing to change her role in the successions of possessions which she will undergo.

43

music that they also enter into trance. Their movements become compulsive; their heads jerk and eyes glaze over. This self-hypnosis comes from the insistent and repetitious beat of the drum, which pushes the musician into realms where he, too, shouts and gasps for breath. This further stimulates the ritual dancer, the manshin.

Fans

It is inconceivable that Shamanist ritual dancing occur without the use of one or more fans. These fans assist in summoning the spirits from their abode, and they also are used to sweep blessings into the outstretched skirts of patrons.

Fans identify a kut as well. The version most commonly seen is a simple composition with three identical figures attired with white, peaked caps. These are the triplets of the "Birth Grandmother," *Sam-shin Halmoni,* and suggest her power of easing childbirth or assistance in the conception of a son since she herself bore boy triplets, even when looked up in a stone box, according to the traditional account. (Details are given in *Shamanist Folk Paintings: Korea's Eternal Spirits*, also published by Hollym International.) This fan is often referred to as "The Three Buddhas."

Another very commonly seen fan is a large, ribbed or folding fan painted with a group of spirits arranged in a sort of hierarchal fashion. At the center will be the *Chesok* or Shamanist-type of Buddha (the triplet's father), with the Mountain Spirit on one side, and also the South Pole Star

Different fans upon an altar, showing the multiplicity of spirits which can be summoned.

A Siberian shaman's headgear, still the most important part of the costume.

who governs longevity. Others present include three generals to represent the five direction-generals, and the Sea Dragon King. This complete pantheon is explained in the above-mentioned book. These same deities are repeated over and over again in various icon paintings used at kuts.

Colors of Clothing Significant

The color symbolism of the five elements and five directions is ever-present. A manshin may change costume several times during the various segments of a kut, and certainly if she performs more than once in a day. The literary spirits summoned at the beginning prefer light colors such as pale blues or greens. Later the hues become brighter and more violent, such as cinnabar reds, clashing greens and royal blues. The Buddhist King of Heaven (Chesok) requires a long white robe and scarf, with an all-white, peaked hat for headgear. It must come to a sharp point at the top.

The dancer knows ahead of time which spirits she will summon, or at least their general character, so she is dressed with several layers if she expects to be possessed by several spirits in turn. Her assistant will help her strip down the outer layer as the occasion demands. In other words, the manshin can change possession and still continue to dance, shedding the outer costume.

The martial spirits are manifested by

One of the very few examples of a Koguryo gilt-bronze crowns in existence, now in the Pyong-yang Museum. All of the crowns worn by the Shaman-kings of ancient Korea are richer and more refined examples of the symbolic magical functions performed by today's Shamanist headgear.

masculine costumes. Their short felt vests are decorated with brass mirrors, sparkling in the light as the spirit-medium dances, symbolizing power. Golden sequins give a vibrant effect. Their military flags are navy blue, green, yellow, red and white. (These are used for fortuntelling.)

Headgear

After seeing a few kuts, it is possible to know which spirit is possessing the man-shin by the type of headgear worn. Traditional headgear has always been very important in Korea, and received great emphasis during the Yi dynasty (1392-1910 A.D.). Perhaps the major role of headgear, more important than in most countries, may reflect the ancient, deep-rooted Shamanist background. The complex, golden crowns of Silla are an early evidence of the sym-

bolic meaning eminating from headgear.

Just as the shaman-king of ancient Silla was endowed with an elaborate crown, even today a performing shaman will have unusual and complex headdresses, far more complicated than one would expect considering her low economic station. The hat, with its feathers, is among the most important parts of a shaman's costume in Korea. The great generals like a red hat made from tiger's fur. A certain kind of hat and chin strap characterize the Great Overseer or Taegam. This is a felt hat which looks like a minor official's hat, with the beads dangling below the chin.

Indeed, it can be said that the headgear makes a performance authentic. In present-day Siberia, when Russian sociologists wished to witness a performance by the still-practicing Yakut, Buryat or Tungus shamans, they agreed to perform without their headdresses, so as not to be sacrilegious. (Without the hat, the dance is only a secular dance, the songs are merely songs. Perhaps the feathers are like antenna, summoning the spirits from the world beyond.)

The Altar: From Man to the Spirits

The use of an altar during worship, with sacrifices placed upon it, indicates the willingness of the supplicant to share his boons with the spirits responsible for producing them. This phenomenon is repeated over and over in various ancient as well as modern religions, with the most notable modern examples of ritual sacrifices upon an altar taking place in Asia.

The altar commonly used in Korean Shamanist rituals differs from those seen in Buddhist rites in that Buddhist altars have a single level. For all its deities, to which the supplicant would pray, are heavenly spirits. Shamanism's heavenly, earthly and underworld spirits receive different types of favorite repasts. One would not place a meat offering before Buddhist spirits, even those with Shamanist leanings, for a part of the conservative Buddhist canon forbids the eating of meat.

A kut which invokes the spirits from all levels will need to have three levels, with offerings tailored to the likes and dislikes of the deities of heaven, earth and underworld. The altar for heavenly spirits consists of sweetmeats (sweetened rice cakes or nut-filled cakes), fresh fruits and nuts, as well as cooked rice. The altar dedicated to the

An altar for a Hwanghae-style kut, held at Korea's National Theater.

Kim Kum-hwa, wearing the monk's hat which indicates the presence of the Chesok Buddha.

A manshin in trance, oblivious to all other things, at the beginning of the *chaktu kori* ("Dancing on the Knives").

earthly spirits will also have fruits, but the grains will be uncooked, with rice being foremost. However, other grains can be used as well. The spirits of earth also demand cooked vegetables and rice cakes as part of the sacrifice, along with the usual offering of uncooked grains and wine.

The underworld spirits like meat most of all, becoming infuriated if they are denied such offerings. The messengers from the underworld (and the hungry ghosts) have a separate altar from the principal meat offering, which is dedicated to *Yomna*, king of the underworld. This separate altar will have "poor foods," such as broken beans and fat, deemed suitable for the lower denizens of the underworld.

It is not always necessary to have all the altar levels ready. Different types of offerings indicate which spirits are expected. However, surprise visits of other spirits do occur. Sometimes the attendants have to scurry around for wine, for example, if the Great Overseer appears. He demands wine!

Dancing on Knives

The best known event in a long kut is the moment in a martial segment when the manshin dances on the edges of sharpened knives. This rite has a long history and has been widely practiced in the Far East. The shamans at the Taoist center of Lu-Shan

48

The manshin is now totally ecstatic, pressing the blades into the soft flesh of her forearm.

Second stage: Knife-riding general, possessing the manshin, demonstrates invulnerability to sharp steel.

(believed to protect China from evil spirits in the northeasterly direction) seem to have specialized on this dance, but with the knives placed on a vertical ladder. Constructing a thirty-foot ladder with sharpened swords for steps is recorded in Chinese histories. During the Sui dynasty (591-608 A.D.) Buddhist monks, in their battle for a following against Taoism's strength, are recorded as climbing seventy-two knives in determined competition with Taoist-Shamanism. This "ladder" represents in a symbolic way the ladder to heaven which the shaman performer ritually climbs to be closer to the heavenly spirits.

In Siberia, the shaman climbed up a white birch tree to be nearer to heaven. In Korea today, a double-edge chopper is used, a pair of blades strapped together with white cloth.

The Koreans present in the audience accept this dancing on knives as proof of the supernatural abilities of the top manshin, but the Westerner tends to be more skeptical and search for a "trick." Perhaps the knives aren't really sharp? While having lunch with some manshin and paksu at their headquarters building, this author tested the blades for sharpness as inconspicuously as possible. A cut rewarded my skepticism.

Manshin facing in the westerly direction as she invokes the Guardians of the Five Directions. The water-filled clay urn which represents clouds in the heavens, the earth, and the ocean is visible supporting the chaktu blades.

Opposite: A manshin licking the sharpened edge of the *chaktu*. As this writer can attest, there was no fakery or trickery involved. The pressure of the tongue can be seen on the edge of the blade; no blood appeared.

Facing north, the first direction to be propitiated. In all this time, the shamaness showed not the slightest discomfort from these steel footpaths through the spirit world.

Yes, those blades are sharp! In fact, a dancer will not perform upon them if they are dull. Nor will the manshin step upon them in stocking feet, but only barefooted.

A missionary offered this author the explanation that "to perform the trick, there must be heavy calluses upon the feet. If the skin is cut," he said, "by all the laws of nature, blood must flow." Of course science cannot admit the possibility of inexplicable things in the realm of the magico-religious.

This explanation of callus might suffice for the fire-walkers of the south seas, whom the doctor insisted walked upon coals that were not really as hot as they looked to the audience, but it hardly accounts for Korea's dancing on knives. The Shamanist believers explain that when possessed by the generals, no blood flows from cuts. In a state of trance, the heartbeat is slowed and blood circulation may be reduced. It is possible to slow one's heartbeat by mental control. But what is happening during the possession of the Korean shaman?

Smoking four cigarettes at once. This act within the ritual may date back to the time when shamans swallowed live coals to demonstrate their mastery of fire, Samgak-san, Seoul.

Illustrated on page 48, is a manshin in trance. Before actually dancing on the knives, she pressed them against her arm, where they left only a slight pressure mark, then against her cheek, where they also left a slight red mark from the pressure. After this, the shaman licked the entire edge of one of the blades with her outstretched tongue! Now, neither her tongue, cheek, or arms could have been protected by old, thick calluses, so the missionary doctor's explanation is inadequate. The saying "mind over matter" comes to the fore. The manshin is no longer in a normal state, but in an altered state of consciousness, so the

ordinary rules concerning physical processes are changed.

At one Full Moon Kut, KBS was present with their telephoto lenses trained on the feet of the manshin as she danced on the knives, which had been placed on top of a water-filled earthen vessel covered with white cloth, symbolizing earth, the sea and clouds in heaven. The lens proved that there was no trickery involved in the dance. Later Korean Broadcasting System put on a program concerning mudang case studies which involved testing by cardiograms and electroencephalgrams. The conclusion that emerged, according to the medical experts, was that "when not in trance, the shamans were normal individuals of average I.Q.," but what happened during a kut was beyond medical detection.

The youngest manshin in Korea, presently age twelve, is an expert at dancing on knives. The knives do not even leave a pressure mark on her flesh. She is shown in a quiet pose on the back cover or dust jacket of this book, but this author has seen her perform on the knives. Being lighter in weight than the older women, she can leap quite high up off the blades and turn different directions in mid-air. Dancing on these knives involves the four cardinal directions and the dancer must face all four ways in turn, first northwards, as the most honored direction.

Lighted Cigarettes

Another seeming trick which sometimes comes during the martial sequence can be termed "smoking four cigarettes simultaneously." To accomplish this, the dancer takes four cigarettes which her assistant has placed in a row and lighted. The manshin then puts all four cigarettes between her lips, puffing once or twice to make them glow red. She then reverses the direction of the cigarettes in her mouth, so that they are

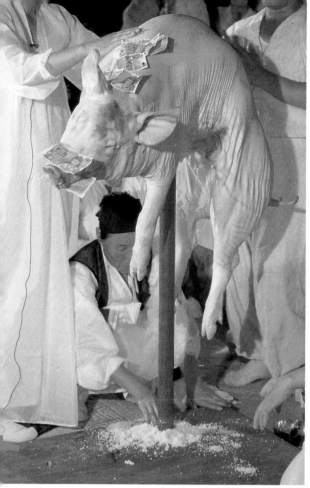

Steadying the pig offering upon the pillar of heaven; if the pig stands upright without tipping, the spirits accept the offering.

A manshin from North Korea steadying the meat offering. This pig tipped over, necessitating a *chaktu kori* (appearance of the Knife-riding General) to drive away the evil spirits which made the flesh of the offering unacceptable.

facing inwards, proceeding to smoke them backwards, with the fiery ends in her mouth. (All of this is done while her dance continues.) The manshin then removes the still-lit cigarettes from her mouth, puffs on them and continues her dance.

The exact meaning of this part of the ritual escapes the author, but it occurs during particularly frenzied martial dances. This type of smoking may hearken back to the practices of Siberia's master shamans, who would put live coals in their mouth to demonstrate their mastery over fire.

The Sacrificial Pig

Large-scale kuts involve the presence of a huge porker, weighing up to three hundred pounds. Smaller kuts have only a pig's head on the altar. Occasionally a cow's head is used (See photo). In theory the animal should be perfect, but exceptions occur. One huge Cholla Namdo kut for many hundreds of people was successful even though an ear had been nicked in the killing so that the country people referred to it as "The kut of the one-eared pig."

A strong desire exists that a kut be considered "successful." Yet the pig ritual seems to be performed against heavy odds. Traditional protocol demands an almost

A Hwanghae province-style kut, with the pig steamed and dismembered, stacked in sections upon the pillar of heaven (a takeoff of the Cosmic Tree).

impossible feat. The carcass of a porker weighing between two and three hundred pounds, after being dressed out, is supposed to balance in a free-standing, horizontal position on top of a single pole about three feet high and an inch and a half in diameter. Sea salt is packed around the base, presumably to invoke the spirits of the sea as well as those of the land in keeping the pole upright. Does a single, vertical pole harken back to the sacred tree of Siberian Shamanism?

At one kut for many people, several shaman-dancers tried to coax the spirits to accept a huge pig, but without success. It would not balance on the slender pole. The kut was then declared a "failure" unless it could be rescued by an appearance of the Knife-riding General. He then possessed a manshin, driving away the evil spirits as she danced upon the knives under his commands. The kut was then termed a success and the pig's carcass was carried out to a roasting pit.

At another kut for hundreds of people including Korea Broadcasting System's television crews, several shaman tried to coax the pig's huge carcass to stay balanced without success. Various members of the audience placed paper money on top of the sacrificial pig's nose, but to no avail. Then the manshin Kim Kum-hwa stepped forward. With her spiritual powers she steadied the pig, invoking the spirits to assist her. When the huge animal did balance on the slender pole for a few seconds, the ritual was declared a success.

Divination or the "Will of the Spirits"

Some mudang practice fortunetelling or divination in their home and do not attempt to put on lengthy kut. Others use some forms of divination as part of a long ritual which is primarily dancing. All these divinations are based on the caprice or the feelings of the spirits at the time a question is asked or expected. (The deities then decide; thus humans are relieved of responsibility for events or even the emotional burden of deciding.)

For example, the attempt to make the sacrificial pig balance upright on a single pole as mentioned previously is a form of Shamanistic divination. A pole, a spear or a sword may be used in a balancing act. If the verticality remains, it is a sign that the spirits are favorable. If it falls down, the spirits are displeased in some way. It very often happens that the "bad sign" occurs, at which point the family that is paying for

A manshin in the personna of a Taegam (overseer) spirit, carrying the cooked pig's head amongst members of the participant-spectators.

a kut is asked to contribute more money to please the spirits. However, if the spear or sword or whatever stands upright (even a few seconds is considered a "good sign"), then the patrons are asked to thank the spirits by placing more money on the altar.

This same principle of favorable or unfavorable movements is used in other ways, such as burning paper (along with a prayer). If the ashes float upwards, it is a good sign, for health and good fortune, but if they move downward, the forecast is negative.

In some cases, paper is rolled into a tube, one per each family that is a patron, and this is burned with the appropriate offerings of foods and wine. In this case, too, the ashes are to first ascend in order to bring a good future.

Numerology is also used for fortune-telling. A favorite method is employing pine tree seeds that have wings. The mudang shakes her container and the number that do not fly out is then counted. (This counting may also be done with sticks or coins.) In every case, an uneven number is fortuitous and an even number is bad. (This harkens back to yang, the heavenly or male component being an odd number and um, the earthly or female component, being an even number in the cosmological system.)

A much used form of divination is with Chinese coins, employing the *I-Ching*. This is a diluted form of Shamanism, probably developed during the Yi dynasty when the *I-Ching* was very popular.

A male shaman, or *paksu* performing in a northern Korean style kut at the Hyatt Hotel, 1981.

4 PRESENT DAY SHAMAN RITUALS AND CUSTOMS

Modern Persecutions

During the early twentieth century, Shamanism in Korea was persecuted by the Japanese, who tried to substitute their own branch of this ancient religion, which Japan had mixed with emperor worship and termed "Shinto," or "Way of the Spirits." Korea's colonial masters thought they would instill loyalty to Japan within the Koreans by emphasizing worship of the sun goddess, along with her descendant, the present emperor Hirohito.

In spite of these tactics, kuts were held in secret. Meanwhile, educated scholars from Japan researched as to why this primitive faith could exercise such a hold over the Korean psyche.

Korea's first president, Syngman Rhee, converted to Christianity and having a European wife, felt no sympathy for native Shamanism. In addition, Park Chung Hee, when president of Korea for eighteen years, actively supressed Shamanism, especially during his early tenure. He felt a "primitive superstition" did not fit in with the stereo-

A lantern which hangs from the branches of a tree which embraces the sacred rock, in the manner of male and female.

type of industrializing Korea that was his ideal. Even so, President Park failed to completely stop the kuts. They were held in secret in the countryside, although broken up by the police in Seoul.

However, in a subterranean fashion, this religion continued in spite of opposition from Korea's better organized religions. Even the word "Shamanism" could not be capitalized, since it was considered superstition and not a religion.

The Fifth Republic is more open to studying and retaining Korea's ancient cultural roots. Thus kuts can be publically mentioned. Recently there have been announcements of Shamanist performances listed in the English language newspapers in Seoul. These include kuts held at places like Korea House, the Space Theater and even provincial performances. Modern, five-star international luxury hotels now hold *kosa* to initiate construction or mark the completion of renovation.

It would seem that a grudging acceptance of Shamanism as part of Korea's cultural

A *kosa* ritual held at the Chosun Hotel on September 4th in 1981. Here Bob Chamberlin of the executive staff can be seen bowing before the altar. Even though this hotel is owned by one of the biggest chains in the hotel business, they followed local custom when a kosa was deemed appropriate at the end of the 12 million dollar renovation projects.

heritage is beginning. (This will be further discussed in Section II on page 104). The present policy of the south Korean government contrasts sharply with the total suppression of Shamanism in north Korea.

Shamans Perform on a Sacred Mountain

In northeastern Seoul, along the wooded slopes of Mount Samgak, long considered a sacred mountain to protect the capital against evil influences from the northeast, is located a three-story building with eight rooms where kuts or segments of kuts are held. Sometimes there is one large kut performed outdoors, on the wooded terrain in front of a huge rock which represents the Mountain Spirit. Other times half a dozen or so ceremonies may be going on simultaneously inside the building, for this is the headquarters of a "Mudang Association." It claims over 70,000 members throughout the entire country, but most live around Seoul or in the central part of Korea.

Shamanistic activities happen here on Samgak Mountain from about nine or ten am. to eight pm. daily, except for taboo days when it is quiet. Ceremonies are especially frequent around the time of a full moon. Live white chickens clutter the hallways; music resounds from each room. On the hill above is a small building, a shrine to the Mountain Spirit. In the basement rooms a fortuneteller may be working; perhaps he is not up to the proficiency demanded by a regular kut.

The dancers who are the "star performers" come from as far away as Inchon or Taegu at the request of patrons. Most of the events fall into the pattern of northern-

Korea's most sacred mountain to Shamanists, called Paektu-san, literally "Whitehead Mountain." This is the legendary site on which Hwanung, the Son of the King of Heaven, descended to Earth. Here also is the birthplace of Tangun, Korea's traditional founder and First Shaman. The present "monarch" (Kim Il-sung) of North Korea often poses on the side of this mountain, showing his "dominance of Korea" in a very Shamanistic manner, while North Korean residents thank him "for making the rain fall and the sun shine." His propoganda machine makes him sound like an old-time Shaman-king, with power over the heavens, able to bend them to his will.

type Shamanism, but the Trip to Hell sequences were heavily influenced by Taoism from China. The cost of such kut is unknown, but a professor of the University of Hawaii, who attended seventeen days in succession last summer, has estimated that an entire day costs a patron or patroness about $1,500. However, various of the spirits who attend, especially those straight from Hell, often demand additional money before they agree to leave. Thus the cost can double or even triple before the rituals are completed. A group of family members or relatives may join together to bear the cost of a day-long performance. It is known that Korea Broadcasting System paid $3,000 each for the rights to film the 1981 and 1982 Full Moon Kut.

58

Altar and sacred rock on Samgak mountain, the headquarters of a 70,000 strong mudangs' union.

Potential of "Ten Thousand Spirits"

The potential guest list exceeds ten thousand, for there are countless spirits in the atmosphere. The top shamans are called manshin, which means, literally, "ten thousand spirits" or one capable of reaching that vast number. Many will come at the summons of a drum and cymbals. In prehistoric times "Ten Thousand Spirits" or manshin was a high title signifying a shaman's unusual ability to summon countless spirits, but today their position is lowly. (See the second section of the book for further discussion of this point.) Various shaman have their favorite spirits whom they prefer to "invite." Also individual manshin specialize in one or another type of calling the spirits and only the best ones are capable of doing a complete cycle such as is encompassed from early morning until dark. A group will go together and each agrees on which part of the day she or he will perform. Few will attempt all the roles required in an eight-hour drama of the spirits.

The basic structure of a kut performed on Cheju Island or around Pusan will be

Separate Mountain Spirit shrine on Samgak mountain. Even though the Mountain Spirit still lives within the rock behind the altar, this separate shrine with a painted icon is a place for a multitude of prayers as well.

The Chinese characters for manshin or "ten thousand spirits."

somewhat different from those going on in the woods. Seoul rites are a combination of Korean Shamanism's northern inheritance (via Siberia and Manchuria) plus Tao-Shamanism's hell sequence which migrated into Korea from northeastern China. It probably took centuries for the present form to evolve.

Four basic segments can be seen enclosed within the fundamental structure which repeats daily. The names of the spirits who put in an appearance vary slightly from day to day, but there are certain "repeaters." Each of the four basic segments fulfill specific functions. Each spirit has its own ambivalent attitude towards the welfare of those human beings who seek help. Each spirit has its area of power; one would not ask a hell spirit for a bountiful crop of children, nor would one expect a literary spirit to actively persecute humans.

Normally each spirit has its particular niche, so to speak, when he or she puts in an appearance, but there might be some crossing over and unexpected appearances of martial or ancestral spirits, since they were once human and are more easily reachable by the suppliants.

One can compare a day's kut to a four-act drama, a single act taking about two hours' time. Before the present noise-abatement laws, kut were put on all night rather than all day.

Time Span of a Kut

The word kut is applied rather loosely to the performance of a spirit-medium. Thus such events or religious services can last anywhere from three to seven days in the community-oriented type of Shamanism prevailing in the extreme south of Korea and be as short as an hour or two if just a segment is seen in Seoul. When performances are scheduled for tourists, such as at Korea House, only parts of several kuts are included, since without understanding the words or the pictorial symbolism, it can be boring.

For those seriously interested, the author recommends the Shaman Headquarters at Mount Samgak, which is within a few minutes taxi ride of the Pugak Tunnel. This area has been sacred to the gods since no one knows when, since "evil spirits" come in most strongly from the northeast and this Samgak Mountain guards the capital city of Seoul from the northeast.

Witnessing even one segment will probably tire the beginning student, as each section lasts an hour or two and the music, although in a different beat from acid rock, is, nevertheless, capable of the same hypnotic effect. Very few Westerners have the hardihood to witness an entire day's program.

Perhaps only a very rare lover of musok will stay down south for the three to five day usual program. Since these agricultural communities in the south have much less distraction and less to break the routine of life, a Shamanistic performance of that duration can be a big festival for those people.

If the reader wishes to adventure to the mountains and is alone, or with a Korean friend, he or she will be welcomed. (Go provided with several 1,000 *won* bills which can be dispersed into the performer's apron when necessary.) It is the most dramatic theater available in the Seoul area. . . at least the most distinctive and indigenous. The theater show at the Sheraton Walker Hill is not too different from New York or Paris, but Mount Samgak is a distinctly Korean species of theater, and it is psychodrama. For the timid, the morning sessions are recommended. For the more adventurous-seeking, the afternoon or early evening. There is a somewhat cumulative effect and

A Manshin in the role of Taegam, whose every movement is followed by the Korean Broadcasting System.

the latter part is more dramatic, more active and engages the services of the most qualified mudangs. In a sense, the most talented manshin COULD accomplish all four segments, but it is a very demanding performance to do solo, so a number of spirit-mediums divide up the dancing segments, and the musicians also change off. It seems as though some mudangs tend to specialize on one or the other segment.

Private patrons who go to Mount Samgak are paying a great deal—perhaps thousands of dollars U.S. for what the foreigner may witness and be asked to contribute a few thousand won bills. It is said that the "spirits" do not like cameras, particularly when television crews clamber all over and approach within inches of the performer's throat or feet while "dancing upon the knives." However, when totally in a trance, the dancer is not aware of these intruders from the non-believing world.

Recently, with renewed interest in Korea's ancient roots, television has become increasingly desirous of introducing at least short segments of kuts to its Korean audience. Since the roots of Shamanism are far more ancient than Shakespeare, or Chaucer, or medievel-mystery plays, closer to Beowulf, to be specific, it is difficult to gauge the

61

A typical altar spread at Samgak mountain, this level of the offerings is for the Earth Spirits.

reaction of the 1980's audience, caught up as it is in Korea's economic miracles.

It can be stated flatly that the most skilled manshin does not go into trance without communicating with the presence of the gods. Before her performance, she hangs up (or her assistants do this chore) some of the portraits that she owns of Shamanistic deities, and then she "invites" their presence to bless the kut. The chief dancer salutes the various deities with brief bows.

These portraits of the spirits, which will be discussed in *Shamanist Folk Paintings*: *Korea's Eternal Spirits* (this book also published by Hollym), become an integral presence for the kut. The sweet cakes, the water-

melon and other fruits which decorate the altars are consumed at the end, but the icons will be reused.

These portraits of the deities or spirits upon which the performer depends, deserve a closer look. Although in theory no hierarchy exists, each spirit having a special area of expertise or efficiency. The above-mentioned book will take a long look at those spirits which are most often summoned to possess a manshin via a portrait and felt to be most effective in this, the twentieth century. Of course, they are all under "The Heavenly Spirit," but that is a separate matter.

5 FOUR BASIC SEGMENTS OF MOUNT SAMGAK PERFORMANCES

The first ritual of the day involves calling the literary spirits of the past. This is the easiest, gentlest section. (It should be mentioned that at the beginning Hananim, the chief Heavenly Spirit, is saluted by the lighting of candles and incense before the altar dedicated to the Heavenly Spirits.) The four parts progress in difficulty, with the ancestral spirits summoned in the second segment. Then lunch is served (after the food has been blessed); then later in the afternoon the third section summoning the martial spirits is put on. Finally, about dark, the Trip to Hell occurs. This involves possession of the manshin by demonic spirits who can cause actual physical danger to the altar, the room itself, or even threaten the onlookers with physical harm, as

Manshin as literary spirit near the beginning of lengthy rites.

well as wearing out the medium. This last segment may be omitted if not needed.

Literary Spirits

Usually a kut begins around ten am. after about an hour spent arranging foods on the altar and setting out other properties, as well as checking costumes and musical instruments. The Literary Spirits are those figures familiar in legend or history. Famous officials from past dynasties of both Korean and China may come, or other benign spirits of the dead past. The "Elder Brother of the Seven Stars" (the Big Dipper) seems to be chief among the literary spirits who appear. Sometimes it will be children cut off in their prime, who later became powerful spirits. One characteristic is that there will seldom be violent, martial beings present.

Hogu, a female spirit formerly personifying Smallpox may come, asking the audience for cosmetic money to cover her pockmarked face. These pits can also be likened to the stars in the sky, or beauty marks. Choyong, the Spirit Guardian against Plague, dates back to poetry of the Unified Silla dynasty.

This early segment is when the patrons will ask for boons to be granted. The "God of Literature" may be invoked to help a son pass a university entrance examination. If, hopefully, a son is about to be born, the "Birth Grandmother" (*Sam-shin Halmoni*) will be entreated so that the birth will be an easy one. This also may include good luck in business and general health for the family.

Ancestral Spirits (*Chosang*)

The segment of a Samgak Mountain kut that summons the ancestors of its patrons is more involved than the beginning rituals to purify the altar and welcome the Literary Spirits. This second segment usually ends peacefully, but it can become grim at mo-

Possessed by the shade of an ancestor.

The ancestor scolding a still-living descendant for foolishly loaning money which was not repaid.

ments if restless and disgruntled ancestors appear through the medium and voice their unhappiness. Sometimes the manshin in possession weeps copious tears when possessed by an unhappy Ancestral Spirit.

A multiplicity of causes could be responsible for raising this wrath, but primarily it is what the shades classify as "improper treatment" by their living descendants. Failing to put the ancestor's favorite dish upon the altar during a *Chusok* festival (memorial day for the ancestral spirits and a harvest holiday), neglecting the careful tending of a gravesite, or having it located in the wrong direction from a geomantic point of view—any of these unfilial acts could arouse the ire of an ancestral shade, thereby bringing grief or misfortune in some form upon the living descendants.

For five hundred years, the dominant religion of Korea was Neo-Confucianism,

Kim Kum-hwa as an ancestral spirit, giving advice through an American disciple mudang from U.C.L.A. faculty.

which emphasized proper worship before the ancestral tablets and extreme care in the selection of a gravesite, but centuries before Shamanism also had prescribed rites to the ancestors to prevent calamity in the lives of the living. Thus Confucianism simply reinforced Shamanistic practices, yet did not include such persons as spirit-mediums to help solve the psychological, medical and emotional problems of the living.

In these ancestral rituals, the manshin is dealing with wandering ancestral shades, not with souls already in Hell. These ancestors are entitled to *chesa* or "feast foods." Usually the ancestors are satisfied after some attention is paid to them and their complaints are adjusted.

When the manshin becomes possessed by an ancestral spirit, she first must identify whom it is that has appeared at the kut, as the patron or family rarely realizes who is causing its problems. Trouble may be due to a close relative, or perhaps a deceased mother or father, who is angered by the behavior of a daughter-in-law. Or it might be a quite distant relative, such as one who died abroad, alone among strangers, who went to the grave without the traditional rites. Souls that committed suicide or died from an accident are often unhappy and particularly restless. They may cause illness in the living until properly assuaged. In this rite the tearing of cloth symbolizes the tearing of the ties which keep the ancestor bound to this world. Throwing millet also is considered appropriate to placate these wandering souls.

Sometimes the wandering spirits of the dead are mild and only offer grandfatherly advice to the patron (via the medium); at other times, the spirits curse and rave at the living descendants, once they have taken possession of the medium. Conditions may

be laid down which must be met before the deceased ancestor will cease to torment the living. The manshin will scold the patrons and tell them what to do. It is assumed that many troubles within the household are caused by displeasure felt by the Ancestral Spirits.

Chesa, the feast foods, have been prepared on an altar and the spirits may enjoy these special delicacies. Then the departed will make peace with the living, who care enough to have ordered a kut for the sake of their ancestors. After the Ancestral Spirits have departed and the manshin has assumed her normal state, the living may partake of the substance of the food, since the ancestors have enjoyed its essence. Also the food is now "blessed" or lucky.

Woman suppliant adding to the offering on the altar.

It is now time for a late lunch, which has been prepared by the kitchen staff at the Mudang Headquarters. Presumably the family that is paying for the kut that day has provided the ingredients. In any case, all the dancers and musicians are fed.

Martial Spirits

After the lunch break, around two pm., the third segment of the long drama begins. In physical terms, this may be much more active than the morning performances, because the generals are being summoned; they are all male. (Chinese poetry which has survived from the second century B.C. has female shamans in love with male spirits

Possessed by the spirit of a general.

and historically some sexual overtones seem to have been involved.)

Martial spirits drive away evil influences and troublesome spirits which have placed stumbling blocks in the patron's path. The generals are also the ones invited when an exorcism is needed. Their swords or knives are necessary symbols to frighten out the demon inhabiting the sick person.

During this segment, the activity of the manshin may become frenzied. Some shiver and shake; others wildly brandish knives as they perform dances which it would seem only a contortionist could copy.

The heavyweights of the martial world, such as the Knife-riding General, the Red Soil Horse General, the White Horse General, the Fire General and the Lightning General are among favorite spirits involved. It takes a strong and sane soul to handle these martial spirits. Manshin may pay a price for having these spirits possess her, such as weakness on schizophrenia if she gets "stuck" in a possession. Many of them sink to the floor from exhaustion at the end of this segment.

Rituals for the Dead and a Trip to Hell

Influence of Buddhism

In the Seoul area, rituals for the dead soul still produce colorful events, rather full of violent action in contrast to Buddhist funerals which consist mainly of a group of

The manshin cutting away evil influences while personifying an historic general.

A grand procession for the king in a Koguryo tomb painting of the fourth century. As in life, so it is in death, the Shamanist belief was that the afterlife was the same as the real world.

monks chanting an appropriate scripture. (The *Amitabha Sutra*, the *Diamond Sutra* or the *Ksitigarbha Sutra* are considered particularly efficacious for the progress of the dead soul.)

It can be said that Shamanistic rites contain indigenous qualities as well as bits of both Mahayana Buddhism and Religious Taoism. Indeed, prehistoric Shamanistic attitudes towards the dead were relatively simple: the afterlife was similar to life on earth; this was combined with a desire to satisfy the dead soul so that it would not bother the living. However, over the centuries, this native attitude has become overlain with the complexities of imported religions. Taoist concepts of a King of Hell with various levels and "gates" have exerted influence on the indigenous faith; in addition, Buddhism's stress on the needs of the soul when it is "reborn" in accordance with its *karma*, have increased the duties of the dead relatives. Neo-Confucianism entails certain obligations on the living descendants, particularly the oldest son; these last into the third year.

Opposite: A Judge of Hell. Chinese Religious Taoism strongly influenced Korean Shamanist beliefs concerning the afterlife.

Scenes from Hell in a Buddhist painting. A damned soul's evil deed (killing a cow with a sledgehammer) is reflected in the mirror.

Shamanism is relatively simple; a single kut can dispose of the contamination brought by death, or the possible evil which lurks, assisting the dead soul to reach a sort of peaceful resolution which will be permanent; thus the living family need not suffer. The present-day ritual has a dual purpose: protect the home and family from death's evil effects and assist the newly dead soul to a peaceful destination in its afterlife.

Different provinces are distinguished by various specially developed kuts, but in the Seoul area, the three main services performed by the manshin or the spirit-medium are to satisfy the dead soul, to remove the evil spirits from the gate of death and to cleanse the family's environment. These rituals require more money than most kuts and a larger display of various foods, placed upon several altars. The most important table is set with offerings for the dead soul; it contains an artificial lotus flower (sacred to Buddhism) tied to a paper effigy, representing the deceased. The King of Hell is given his own offering table, while another is especially reserved for the Buddha and still another for the spirit of the mountain top. Outside or at a distance, a table is set up for the "unclean spirits" and those called "Hungry Ghosts" in Buddhist parlance.

The Judgment Hall (where the ten Kings of hell reside), with portraits of the departed, so prayers can be offered for the rest of ancestors.

The interjection of Taoist ideas as well as Buddhist ideas into this Shamanistic ritual for the dead evidences the long and complex history of Korea's indigenous religion. Siberian Shamanism had spirit-medium who went to the heavenly world, known as "white shamans," while "black shamans" could or would make excursions to the nether world. However, in present-day Seoul, an expert manshin is able to travel (figuratively or spiritually) in either direction—upwards or downwards, so to speak, depending on which spirits are invited or summoned and which spirits choose to take possession of the particular medium on any one occasion. The words of ·the song, the type of music, as well as the movements of the dance, together summon the desired spirits. In other words, a heavenly spirit would not come when certain music is played and a spirit from the underworld would not appear in another type of kut.

In Korea, as in Japan, Buddhism more or less appropriated for itself the major responsibility of caring for the souls of the dead and worked out a series of "possible rewards" for the faithful. Yi-dynasty temples contained (and many still do preserve them) a huge canvas termed "Sweet Dew" which divided the afterlife into an upper section where the "Good" (or devout from a Buddhist point of view) could be seen gathered together with a central Buddha figure and various bodhisattva at the top, but beneath this the scroll showed various demons practicing cruelties such as tearing out the tongue of a liar or sawing in half the body of a two-faced person. The lessons were clear.

From the sixth century in China, the custom had grown up of chanting masses for the dead, on the theory that this would elevate the position of the dead soul in the afterlife. The first forty-nine days were especially important, seven being a lucky number and seven times seven or forty-nine days being the period during which the soul's status at rebirth was determined. This was primarily in accordance with one's *karma*, but it could be improved by the chanting of masses. In Buddhism there were six realms for rebirth; living relatives could help the dead soul through this period of difficulty and judgment.

Shamanism in the central part of Korea seems to have adopted some of these Buddhist ideas of death, but never to have quite lost sight of its earlier concepts, which caused the fabrication of beautiful crowns and horse trappings for its royalty. Korean society always was hierarchical, so the lower-class people were forced to toil to make artifacts for the afterlife of the top class. What happened to the commoner became of little concern. He just died.

Also Shamanism seems to have adopted, over the centuries, the basic geography of Hell as worked out by the Taoists around the fourth to sixth centuries, a period when Religious Taoism was entering Korea. Especially popular were various Taoist rituals and liturgies whereby the living could assist the upwards progress of the dead. Painters working on Taoist subjects vividly depicted the judges of each section of Hell and the horrible punishments in

which the area specialized. Thus the family which ordered a Shamanistic ritual was motivated by both selfish and unselfish thoughts towards a dead relative.

Present-day rituals in Seoul begin with a purification of the altar surroundings, followed by purifying the altar itself symbolically with fire and water. Various gods are sacrificed to, and then the soul of the dead is summoned back by the presence of his or her clothes placed beside the altar. The spirit-medium raises these clothes up and swings them around in the dance, then wraps them around her body as she feels the soul taking possession of her. At this point, the spirit-medium is able to speak with the voice of the deceased.

The family and friends or relatives then converse with the dead, lamenting with loud voices. Finally the angelic spirits take the dead soul away, as the manshin changes her style of dancing. She now holds a white paper in her right hand and a bell in her left hand.

Messenger from the King of Hell

The manshin's body becomes agitated as she changes costume again and wraps two small pieces of white cloth around her forehead. This signifies that the Messenger of the King of Hell has taken possession of the spirit-medium. This messenger, Iljik Saja, is strong and willful. He will attempt to destroy the main altar and also to reach the white paper on the central altar, so that symbolically he can carry the dead soul directly to Hell.

The relatives are expected to guard the altars and protect them from Iljik Saja, for the shamaness, when possessed by him, is extraordinarily strong. The deceased family should attempt to get the Messenger from Hell to eat only at the table laid out with impure foods. The King of Hell himself

72

Walking-on-Nails Hell.

Starving Hell.

Sawing-in-Half Hell (for those who are two-faced).

Boiling Oil Hell.

Freezing Hell.

Hell of Snakes.

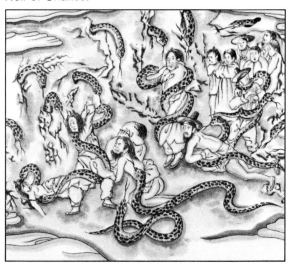

Judgment Hall at Chikchi-sa with the King of Hell, the central figure.

Opposite: Iljik Saja (also known as Woljik saja or by several other names) the Messenger from Hell, who with warrants in hand, drags the soul to judgment.

does not appear. (He is *Yomna* in Korean, *Yen-lo* in Chinese and *Emma* in Japanese. Presumably he is quite busy elsewhere.)

It is noticeable that the altars constructed for the underworld are placed on a lower level than those dedicated to the heavenly or earthly spirits. What may be termed the "Lower Altar" is set with a little cooked food, but its chief centerpiece is meat, either pork or beef, represented by a pig's head or a cow's head. The "unclean altar" should be located outside the room if possible. It will contain raw or fatty meat and rough, uncooked foods such as onions, broken beans, leeks and glutinous rice cakes.

Pali Kongju as Guide to the Underworld

Only physically and mentally strong manshin can undertake a voyage to the lower world. In part of the rite, a small mound of uncooked rice or rice flour is covered with a cloth, a paper representing the dead, then a candle made of waxed, twisted cloth is placed upon it. While the candle burns, the spirit medium recites the story of Pali Kongju, as she has learned it from her teacher. A recital of this narrative takes about half an hour. Each region has a

A shamaness as Pali Kongju, the one who can rescue ancestors from torment in the world beyond.

Pali Kongju, traveling through the arch which signifies the gateway to Hell.

slightly different variant, but all glamorize Pali Kongju as a sort of first ancestress of female shamans.

In all variants, Pali is "the seventh daughter of an ancient emperor." In Chinese legends she was born to an emperor who very much wanted a boy and was disappointed when his seventh child was a girl, like the other six. Finally an eighth child turned out to be a boy, but this son died

shortly afterwards. The seventh princess took it upon herself to go down to Hell and rescue her brother through her extraordinary powers as a shamaness. (After that she has made many trips.)

Another variant, especially prevalent in the Seoul area, is that Pali Kongju's father was greatly angered when she was born, putting her in a stone box and casting it away into a pond. Heaven thereupon sent a

Pali Kongju as a young girl, performed by an apprentice mudang. This kut was more of a theatre type of performance, so the dance and accompanying regimen were not as strict as usual.

dragon-king to rescue her, lifting her up to heaven. The father became ill, so the mother beseeched Pali Kongju to go to the Western Sky to get "medicine water" which would effect a cure.

Pali Kongju labored for nine years in the land of the Western Sky to obtain the medicine water, finally marrying and bearing seven sons to the gatekeeper as payment for the boon. By the time Pali Kongju returned both parents were dead, but the water restored them to life. The central idea of Pali Kongju's ability to rescue others

remains throughout all the varying tales, although the particulars and even the name by which Pali Kongju is addressed changes. At some point in time, probably during the early Silla period, she was selected as the most propitious spirit to summon for this rite (as well as becoming celebrated as the "first shaman" of Korea, from which all others descend).

Confucian ideas concerning filial children dominate the Pali Kongju tales; the rites which seek surcease for the soul wandering in Hell are necessitated by the filial duty of children towards parents. Thus Pali Kongju's Shamanistic abilities make her the natural choice for performing filial services to souls in the afterlife.

After completing the tale of Pali Kongju,

One of the daughters of Pali Kongju, who helped spread Shamanism to the eight provinces of Korea, Author's Collection, Seoul.

Temple painting from Kanghwa Island, showing the criteria by which souls in Hell are judged.

the manshin will lift the cloth which covers the small mound of rice or rice flour, reading the tracks left by the passage of the soul. Those which resemble birds' footprints or butterflies' wings indicate that the trapped soul can fly upwards from Hell. Imprints in the rice which indicate the twisting locomotion of a snake show that the soul is not yet ready for release. No tracks at all in the mound of rice indicate that the soul is confused, wandering aimlessly in Hell and may cause future problems for the family unless it can release the trapped spirit from bondage.

Rescuing the Dead Soul

A shaman's trip downwards seems directed towards the rescue of a certain individual whereas the recitation of a Buddhist sutra accumulates merit for the patron who pays for it, as well as brings relief from suffering to those trapped in Hell. If the soul for which the chant is intended has already been reborn, the chanting adds merit to all unfortunates and the patron's generosity is not squandered but added to his karma.

Ploughing the tongue of a liar, with red-haired
hungry ghosts, Woljong-sa.

Shamanism is more direct, individualized
and less prolonged than Buddhist rites. A
single "rescue trip" suffices for a particular
relative, but it is best performed as soon as
possible after death, even though the funeral
may have been a Buddhist one. After three
years, rescue is very difficult. Shamanism
contains no idea of "overlapping" onto
other souls or of "universal assistance" as
in Buddhism.

Mahayana Buddhism evidences some
thought that the reading of sutra will
instruct the souls in the underworld, guiding
them towards religion and being reborn
with a better karma. In Shamanism the
dead soul is to be directly rescued by a
process of "possessions" by the shaman-
medium, who will become or fight off the
King of Hell's Messenger, or whoever else
tries to cling to the dead soul and prevent
its release. A good deal of money is
required to satisfy these underworld
characters, offerings which revert to the
manshin who BECOMES THEM for a
period of time.

Hungry Ghosts

Much money and food are required for
this ritual for the dead both in Shamanism
and in Buddhism. The indigenous religion
seems to have picked up from Buddhism
the concept of "Hungry Ghosts" (*preta* in
Sanskrit, *Agwi* in Korean). These unfor-

A Hell painting from a Buddhist temple on Cheju Island, with hungry ghosts seen as demons tormenting their captives.

tunates have great trouble in eating because their throats have been constricted to about the size of a pin. In this ravenous state they eat human excrement. On the fifteenth day of the seventh month, these Hungry Ghosts visit earth for three days. This marks the big mid-summer festival (*paekjung* in Korean, *obon* in Japanese).

In Shamanism, extra altars of food offerings are laid out in the ritual for the dead, so that those from the underworld will not try to eat from the food offerings for the heavenly spirits. When the Hungry Ghosts take possession of a manshin, an interesting tableau occurs. As a ravenous creature

from the underworld, she cannot eat in a regular manner, but attacks the food offerings, trying to eat everything in sight. Although an altar table with "unclean food" has been prepared, the possessed medium is not satisfied by that. (Her throat is psychologically constricted during this altered state of consciousness.) She hurriedly stuffs food and wine in her mouth, and then vomits it out, unable to swallow. An assistant follows the medium, holding a pail below the mouth of the possessed one,

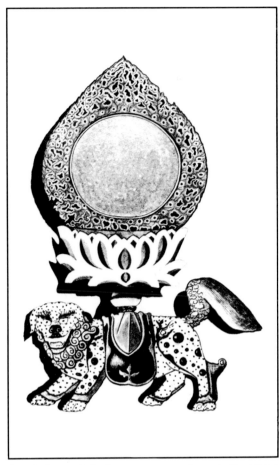

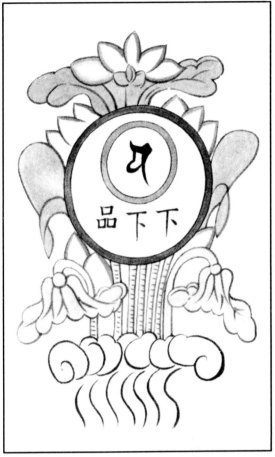

The Mirror of Judgment, even though Buddhist in nature, the "mirror" showing the deeds of the soul, is basically shaman in connotation.

The ninth level of Hell. The two characters, which signify "The bottom under the lowest section" indicate a level that only a grafting official or tyrant king could reach.

trying to catch the vomit. The possessed medium is, of course, unconscious of her behavior.

Cutting the Gates with Swords

The principal dance in the manshin's ritual for the dead, as performed by the ecstatic-type of shaman practicing in the Seoul area, is complex, to say the least. The dance movements are far more intricate than a trip to the underworld performed by Siberian shamans in trance, as described by Russian and French anthropologists. Korea's closeness to China, where Religious Taoism had developed elaborate ideas concerning a ten-level Taoist Hell (in contradistinction to Mahayana Buddhism's "Six Realms of Existence" in the afterlife), probably accounts for this complexity.

Those familiar with the magic diagram created for Taoist Hell can visualize on the floor of the room or on the courtyard if it is held outside, a square consisting of nine chambers. This magic diagram or *mandala*

81

forms a sort of invisible road map for the manshin's journey to Hell.

The shamaness appears to be repeating something within her unconscious, a plan transferred orally, person-to-person or teacher-to-disciple. The icons used by mudang do not have this magic diagram, but its basic structure can be sensed by a knowledge of Taoism's nine chambers.

According to Taoist cosmology, the spirit-medium dances through nine squares, using knives in her hands to cut through the four gates which lead from chamber to chamber underground. These are (according to Taoism) the Gate of Man, the Gate of Heaven, the Gate of Demons and the Gate of Earth.

Since repetition three times is important in liturgy, the shaman-dancer must pass through these nine chambers three times in succession, opening the gates in a symbolic manner. The three times represents the three stages of existence in Shamanism: underworld, earthly world and heavenly world. After the last gate is entered, the soul is released and free to fly towards the Western Paradise (an influence of Pure Land Buddhism and Amitabha's Western Paradise). As an assistant burns a paper effigy, the soul of the dead departs.

It should be mentioned that the four gates are opened by the shamaness' gesture of slashing or cutting; she is equipped with short-handled knives to use in crashing through the four gates. As she dances through the gates, she tosses back the four knives in turn, to be caught by her assistant (each knife used three times). During this segment of the "trip to Hell" the dancer is robed in red and yellow robes, the favorites of Pali Kongju.

Cloth as Bridges

Another colorful feature of this ritual is the use of long rolls of cloth, furnished by the relatives. These serve as symbolic "bridges." The hempen or rough material forms a path to the underworld and the fine muslin a path to Heaven. (There is also an um-yang symbolism here.) As part of the finale the manshin puts on an elaborate wig, with decorative gold and silver hairpins; she dances upon the path created by the textiles now stretched out along the floor. (In trance she must dance with a topheavy headdress.)

During this dance the avariciousness of the Hell Spirits comes out and the relatives must sprinkle much money along the path, for the sake of the dead soul. There is a belief that only officials are permanently kept in Hell and that they are as greedy there as in earthly life.

One northern, ecstatic-type manshin, Kim Kum-hwa, was seen to sweep up these rolls of cloth and entangle them around her head as she continued her ecstatic dance in final celebration of freeing a soul trapped in the underworld.

After the soul has been freed, the exhausted manshin and all the participants thank the spirits for their attendance at the kut, then bid them farewell and a pleasant journey back to their separate realms. Then the foods on the sacrificial altars may be eaten by the participants, even the pig's head.

A "Sweet Dew" painting of the afterlife from Pomun-sa temple on Cheju Island. The nature of the mixture of Shamanist, Taoist and Buddhist beliefs can be seen here. At the rear of the Dragon Boat (Taoist) which carries the souls to the (Buddhist) Western Paradise, is Pali Kongju, whose white cloth bridge (Shamanist) leads the trapped soul to its release from a (combination) Hell.

This zodiac, with its twelve divisions, was the "blueprint" for a person's life in Korea. Before marriage, or any momentous decision, a fortuneteller would be consulted to see what the zodiac would forecast as the outcome.

PART II
SHAMANISM IN PERSPECTIVE

A manshin performing near the turn of the century.

6 SHAMANISM IN KOREA A CENTURY AGO

Scarcity of Information

Shamanism has always been primarily an oral tradition. Since 1392 A.D. it has been actively discouraged and suppressed, so that what records remained for a prior period are no more. A few ideas can be gathered by reading the *Samguk Yusa* of the thirteenth century, but these are merely hints gleaned by sifting through legends attributed to Buddhism. When missionaries arrived in the late nineteenth century, they regarded Shamanism as "pure demonology," but some of them kept records of the rituals used and the "spirits" they saw worshipped.

Needless to say, the missionaries did everything in their power to ridicule and suppress this folk faith. Christianity was the third major religion to look down on and make fun of Shamanism in the Korean peninsula. Yet in spite of the superior airs of Buddhism, the active suppression of Neo-Confucianism and the ridicule of Christianity, at the end of the Yi dynasty, Shamanism probably had more active believers, who sought its shamans in time of need, than the other religions.

Bottom Caste, But Needed

Yi-dynasty society was very class-minded. A century ago, the bottom class in Korea was *Chonmin* into which mudang and paksu were lumped together with slaves, butchers, actors and "ladies of the evening" or *kisaeng*. About fifty different names were current for shamans practicing in Korea, according to region and function. *Yubok* were fortunetellers who did not hold kuts and were considered the least skilled. Mudang was the general name used for musok or the female practitioner of the folk faith which depended heavily on muga,

Male shaman performing in a ritual painting.

or song recitation then widespread in the south of the peninsula. Paksu was but the most common of many names applied to male performers (as opposed to male musi-

86

Male shaman performing at Samgak Mountain.

cians). In this book the polite term of man-shin, or "(Capable of summoning) Ten Thousand Spirits" has been used for a practioner of northern-type ecstatic dance.

In Korea of a hundred years ago, shamans were summoned to perform kuts for the same reasons as in ancient times (and also today). Their chief services included appeasing malignant spirits, curing sickness, forecasting the future and supplicating the spirits for future successes. Mudang and paksu were asked to handle all manners of calamity.

During the Yi dynasty, the influence of Shamanism was not restricted to the lower classes, even if its "priests" were "Chonmin." For example, it is recorded that in the 1890s the last major queen of this dynasty, Queen Min, had a favorite mudang whom she elevated to the official rank of "princess" and attempted to make the Confucian-minded ministers bow before her. (It must have been quite a little drama!)

Home-Centered Folk Faith

Presumably Shamanism remained alive because of the interest of women, more than anything else. These women were barred from taking a leading part in Confucian ceremonies, but they were held responsible for maintaining a smooth flow of events within the home. When instability threatened, arranging for a kut was the normal procedure. In a pre-scientific age before the development of psychology, a kut was the best known remedy. Furthermore, kuts were an acceptable way for women to socialize. Even the upper-class women were confined and only allowed outdoors after a curfew bell held the men

to their houses about 8 or 9 p.m. When a
kut was scheduled, the lofty Confucian
scholar-official might scorn the rituals, but
he would seldom forbid them, especially
when it concerned matters within his own
home.

Before a new house or even a new room
or storage area could be used, a kut would
be held to placate the roof-beam spirit
(*Songju*). Care was taken not to step on the
doorsill, which was considered to be his
neck. Each year at harvest an offering would
be made to this deity, who liked rice, wine
and fruits. If accidents occurred within the
home, it was assumed that Songju had been
neglected in some way.

Neo-Confucian principles demanded that
women give birth to sons in order to carry

Kuksadang shrine, on Mt. Inwang, where women
would pray for male issue.

on the family life. Thus mudang would
hold a kut for the "Three Spirits" (Sam-
shin). This would supposedly ensure that
the child would be a boy and also assist in
safe delivery.

Special kuts and prayers for barren
women. were also practiced. In the trance
state, shamans would prescribe drugs and
potions believed to be efficacious for pro-
moting pregnancy. The EXTREME importance of male descendants made assistance
from a mudang acceptable, especially as a
sort of last resort. In this way Shamanism
was assisting the performance of Confu-
cian-oriented ancestor worship. Few re-

88

An ancient fertility shrine at Chikchi-sa symbolizing procreation, which will be visited by Korean women to pray for a son.

called that in prehistoric times, the worship of ancestors had been conducted by Shamanism; then later Buddhism took over ancestor worship; finally it was Neo-Confucianism that played the main role with Shamanism merely as an "assistant."

General Conditions a Century Ago

Korea could be classified as in an advanced agrarian stage eighty or a hundred years ago; thus it had all the rituals surrounding planting and harvest that this state implies. A *Todang Kut* was held for a rich harvest or the welfare of the entire village; this normally was performed by the local village mudang. These spirit-intermediaries were not of the type "called" by a certain spirit, but had acquired their knowledge and position through heredity. Such country shamans did not have individual patrons, like those in the large cities, but usually served several farming villages (the *tangol* system), coming when needed. They were paid by collecting rice in a manner similar to a tithe, with the amount per year fixed for each family, unless it needed special emergency services, at which time extra was paid.

In the outlying areas, kuts were performed at pre-set times; in case of disaster they occurred more frequently. The most vital occasions were rain-begging ceremonies. Such kut could last for days, cen-

Hillside shrine

tering around an iconographic painting representing the rain dragon. More than one shaman would take part in these important rituals; at times even especially powerful shaman from the bigger cities were solicited to assist, since success was so important to a region when most life was basically agri-cultural.

As in ancient times, spirits of the dead were among the principal fears of individual Koreans. Kuts were held on many occasions related to death, or where people had met violent deaths, such as drowning or having been eaten by a tiger. At certain times each year, in order to placate the malignant river ghosts, ceremonies were conducted by one or more shamans, on all the major rivers, as well as at the important ports in Korea. The spirits of unmarried women, or those who had died childless were considered especially dangerous, so ceremonies were held at their death to ensure that they did not try to take from the living the husbands or children which they had been denied during interrupted lives.

At the close of the Yi dynasty, Shamanism permeated almost every breath that Korean women inhaled. Advice from the spirits was asked on all matters of importance and protection against evil influences was always sought. Every event was considered as happening due to the influence of spirits. No square inch of the home was free from their malicious mischief if the spirits felt neglected.

By the coming of the twentieth century, Buddhism had assimilated much of Shamanism, and vice versa; Taoism had become thoroughly mixed with both of them. Confucianists had ignored or suppressed the folk faith even more than it had Buddhism, and yet the strains of Siberian-type ecstatic Shamanism remained in the north while the agrarian type remained paramount in the south. Mudang performing a kut were still the best way to communicate with the spirit world, to obtain a forecast of the future or to strive for wish-fulfillment and overcome negative events. It has been estimated that almost every Korean woman believed in Shamanism, and a large proportion of the men outside of the official class.

90

Above: A springtime festival on the Han River, with two rituals, one Buddhist, one Shamanist. The ritual to the Shamanist Dragon King is shorter, but the devotion seems more intense.

Below: A suppliant throwing "mulgogi pap" (millet treated with sesame oil) to the fish in the river, in hopes that the wishes which accompany the offering will reach the Dragon King of the River.

7 SHAMANISM'S ROLE IN MODERN-DAY KOREA

Shamanism is currently undergoing somewhat of a revival due to recent efforts to reconstruct Korea's cultural "roots" before they disappear under the march of industrialization. However, due to the communist dictatorship in north Korea and its suppression there of Shamanism (along with Buddhism and Christianity), the ecstatic-state type of mudang has become much less numerous. Today Seoul boasts a Headquarters Building at Mount Samgak for an organization that claims 70,000 dues-paying members. Many of the kut described in this book were witnessed there. It is noticeable that few kut are performed in private homes any more, particularly in the capital area. Noise-abatement laws have also been influential.

This is not to say that rituals of a sort are totally neglected even in the heart of Seoul with almost nine million people and all kinds of "modernisms." Within the past year two deluxe hotels of international reputation have held shaman rituals to celebrate some sort of "opening." The Hyatt Regency scheduled a *kosa* to celebrate the opening of two, refurbished private dining rooms on its second floor.

The Westin Chosun, after a $12,000,000 renovation of the entire building, also held a kosa with even more dancing and singing. Due to the extent of the Westin Chosun's renovations, its kosa performers went from floor to floor (The elevator waited for the musical group—a modern touch!), so that all twenty floors were covered, as well as beginning at the parking lot and ending at the rooftop's "Mug Club," where the longest performance went on. At both hotels the managers participated, though obviously somewhat unwillingly or perhaps one should say "sheepishly" as they lighted a candle before the pig's head.

A North Korean style kut held at the Hyatt Hotel.

Dancers at a *kosa* held at Seoul's Westin Chosun Hotel.

The Friendship Bell Pavilion at San Pedro's "Angel's Park," overlooking the harbor of Los Angeles, also had a kut or perhaps just a kosa. (The author wasn't present, but only read newspaper clippings.) The excuse was that the carpenters imported from Korea insisted, but perhaps the consulate personnel from Wilshire Boulevard did not object too strongly.

Live chickens are still being sacrificed at Mount Samgak, used to absorb or draw out the evil spirits. Huge porkers are still being sacrificed, and certain Seoul markets have a whole display area of pig's heads, which someone certainly is buying.

But the future of Shamanism may be as a sort of anachronism, preserved as a cultural treasure from the past more than being the major faith of more than half the population, as in former times.

For one thing, the role of Korean women is changing; they are having careers and deserting the home-as-a-prison. The literacy rate is rising each year, now health courses are compulsory. Modern medical knowledge is accessible to a large proportion of the population today.

Perhaps it is the change in architectural styles that is responsible for a mortal blow directed at the household spirits which once ruled in an unquestioned manner. Furthermore, delivery in a hospital instead of the home has dealt a death blow to the former

93

importance of the Birth Grandmother. More than the ridicule of Christian missionaries, architecture and science, together with a Western-style education, have removed former dependence on a world of "spirits" as an explanation for every event, good or bad.

Furthermore, both Buddhism and Christianity (especially Protestantism as practiced in Korea) have incorporated so many of Shamanism's basic ideas, that the folk religion does not need a separate existence any more, particularly in the large cities where agricultural rites are not needed. The Saemaul Undong Movement, in organizing the farmers, has tried to oppose Shamanism; time will tell how effective it has been.

Modern Architecture Helped to Destroy the Abode of "Spirits"

In previous periods the bulwark of Shamanistic beliefs lay within the traditional Korean home, where the wife was practically a prisoner; her principal relief came through kuts. All upper-class mansions as well as peasant homes possessed an ancestral shrine in the approved Neo-Confucian manner. But according to the mistress, each house also was inhabited by countless spirits of the Shamanistic world. Strange noises in the ceilings or straw roofs could be those spirits manifesting their presence (or they could be rats?). Since the Roof Beam Spirit had become the generalissimo of all the household spirits, it was only prudent to keep him content with food and wine offerings.

Architectural changes begun in the mid-twentieth century brought about the housing of Korea's populations in modern concrete homes in the countryside and in skyscraper apartments with plenty of light in the cities. (Spirits naturally prefer the dark.) This modernization of housing has done

Chesok-Buddha, the Buddhist King of Heaven (and fertility) from a family Confucian type-Shamanist Shrine, formerly near Mapo district in Seoul, now Emileh Folk Art Museum, Songni-san National Park.

much to reduce the concern of the housewife or her needs for appeasing (as formerly) the multi-spirits and their gaggle which inhabited her home and influenced events, according to the native belief.

In the concrete grid of a skyscraper apartment, the Roof Beam Spirit (*Songju*) has no

94

The roof beams of the American Ambassador's residence in Seoul, the habitation of the in-house "roof-beam" spirit.

roof beam for his abode; the Household Official (*Toju Taegam*), who formerly resided at the back of the chimney flue, seems homeless when there is no longer a chimney. The toilet shed, once the traditional home of the toilet spirit, has been banished by modern plumbing, so this deity and his power have met their demise. It is no longer a common custom to set out cups of wine throughout the house (and the outhouse) to satisfy these thirsty spirits. In the remote villages their presence may still be felt, as in olden times, almost as a daily occurrence. But in the large cities such as Seoul (home of more than one out of every four Koreans), it is only at moments of crisis that a family feels the need for an intercessor, or a meeting with the Shamanistic spirits.

Modern Theater Competes with Shamanism's Psycho-Drama

In these days of Hollywood movies or space sagas with fantastic staging and trick lighting, the shaman's flashing knives during "possession" by the martial spirits seem less potent and less dangerous than in more traditional times. The spirit-medium still exorcises the noxious influences for patrons who believe in or are comforted by a kut, but usually they are of the older generation. A few college students are interested in fortunetelling, but not much else.

95

A page from a modern manshin's calendar. The signs of zodiac are on each day, indicating taboo days for certain things or acts which must be avoided on particular days.

Koreans Have Forgotten about "Blocked Directions"

As for "inauspicious days" and "blocked directions," these beliefs also are on the wane. Korea inherited from China's ancient cosmology an almanac of "good directions" and "evil directions" which meant that bad spirits were blocking certain paths of action. This applied particularly to travel, to moving furniture and to other physical acts. It was best one waited; the ninth and tenth days were good.

This whole system was based on the lunar calendar. If moving eastward, the first and second were days of bad direction; if going south, the third and fourth were to be avoided; if going westward the fifth and sixth; the seventh and eighth days were bad for action pointed northward. Only days nine and ten of the cycle were totally safe.

However, modern work schedules cannot accommodate such taboos; subways go in many directions; construction jobs require movement in all directions. The populace at large has come to pay little attention to "blocked directions" or feel that illness necessarily comes from a disregard of this ancient almanac derived from China many centuries ago.

Today there is little talk about "inauspi-

Woodblock print of a Choyong dance amulet, now losing ground to modern medicine.

cious days," except in the remote countryside among the elderly. However, when a wedding day is set, a soothsayer might be consulted about an auspicious day. But this is a major occasion. The concept of good and bad directions no longer effects everyday actions.

Modern Medicine and Science Destroyed the Shamanistic Spirits

The proliferation of hospitals has removed "the pollution of birth" once felt so that the Birth Grandmother (Samshin Halmoni) required special offerings for three days. Mother and child need no longer be isolated for three weeks; this may prove impractical.

Health courses in schools have taught the coming generation to replace the Shamanistic spirits as the cause of illness with such concepts as germs and bacteria. Smallpox

has been eliminated, so what role is left for the disease-fighting spirits? Science courses have placed a distance between the outlook of the younger generation and its parents, or especially its grandparents.

Sexual Overtones within Shamanism

It is very evident, especially during the Yi dynasty (1392-1910 A.D.) that Korean women were so suppressed in a social sense that when asking for a kut they were acting out some of their repressed sexual feelings, striving for temporary escape from the official religion which put them in such a subordinate position within society. The female shamaness was ranked in the bottom class, but when she reached ecstasy, that didn't matter.

The songs of the shamanesses of Chou dynasty China contain references to sexually-tinged ecstatic delights and the female shamaness longing or calling for the male god. When the mudang puts on many layers of male clothing, she is permitting the male over her body, she is receiving his spirit into her body. This is a sort of symbolic sexual intercourse. The receptive moment comes when the trance reaches its peak and a sort of "mystical union" occurs, so that the two become one, the female medium and the male spirit or deity. This mystical union probably surpasses the normal experiences of average conjugal life.

The Shamanistic sickness or shinbyong has been likened to a type of love-sickness, with some similar symptoms such as loss of appetite, dreams or visions and strange behavior, which is not cured until the love is resolved. It is noticeable that the male shaman or paksu usually wears female clothing in his dancing. This is termed "transvestite" in the West, but it would rather seem to be a symbolic union of the two sexes again.

The initiation process of northern-type

Shamanism which prevails in Seoul can be likened to a "wedding with the god," since each manshin has her particular guardian spirit. This is the *Naerim kut*, in which the new spirit-medium is accepted by her guardian spirit. It is interesting that the ecstatic moment is referred to as "*Shin baram*" or literally "wind of the spirits" but the "wind" has a sexual connotation.

After the initiation or "marriage with the deity," the female manshin is expected to offer pure water on her household altar to her particular "god-husband" each morning. A disengagement from normal sex life is frequent as the mystical union with the divine has taken its place. There are exceptions, however. A few manshin seem to regard their husbands with respect and use them as musicians who accompany their dance. One might almost say that women's liberation began in Korea at least as far back as the Yi dynasty when the female shamaness discovered greater ecstasy with a divine husband than with an earthly one. The West has parallels, such as St. Theresa, represented (1650 A.D.) by the famous Italian sculptor Bernini in a pose of "ecstasy" with her spiritual bridegroom, Jesus Christ. St. Theresa in her writings refers to being "a bride of Christ," and a somewhat similar term is used even today when a Catholic nun takes her final vows.

Pioneer Work by Yongsook Kim Harvey

The major definitive work so far published on the personal history of shamans practicing in the Seoul area was a Ph.D. research project submitted to the University of Hawaii by Yongsook Kim Harvey. It has now been printed as *Six Korean Women,* by St. Paul's West Publishing.

This book is a unique, pioneering effort to probe the lifestyles of present-day manshin. It gives lengthy sociological studies, not only of the role of the shamaness in modern Korean society, but how these women feel about their own roles in the social system.

Manshin appear to derive from all walks of life, from the totally illiterate to those with college degrees, as revealed by her book. (One manshin known to this author even holds an M.A. in anthropology!). Some have "rude and crude" country backgrounds; others are somewhat urbane. Three examples have been paraphrased from this pioneering work, copyrighted in 1979, to illustrate the variety of present-day Seoul practitioners.

Pyongyang Manshin

Pyongyang Manshin was born in 1925; she graduated from high school, something rather rare for a girl at the time of the Japanese Occupation. Her birthplace was located north of the 38th parallel; she suffered from shinbyong, the illness sent by the spirits, on four different occasions. After an unstable childhood, she bore nine children (plus three abortions). Pyongyang Manshin was evicted from her mother-in-law's house, but later had to let the woman move in with her.

All the manshin's children did well enough; one even managed to reach the United States. It would appear that she is reasonably happy with her life; she feels that her major function is to reassure people.

Most of the clients that Pyongyang Manshin sees are women, those with problems. Their husbands treat them badly—their children are sick—their mothers-in-law are brutal. This manshin stated that doctors treat people simply as disease-carriers, rather than like human beings. She treats everyone as an individual; this makes the person feel as if she or he mattered. Pyongyang Manshin becomes frustrated over those cases where she can do nothing. Her role presently seems to be that of a quasi-psychologist, but instead of calling on Freud or Jung, she calls on the demigods of Korea's cultural past.

Ttonggol Manshin

Ttonggol Manshin also was born in north Korea, yet in many ways she appears to be the exact antithesis of Pyongyang Manshin. The very name "Ttonggol" means "Shit Alley." It represents the neighborhood in Seoul where she lived after fleeing south during the Korean War (1951).

Ttonggol Manshin is functionally illiterate, but possesses a great deal of native intelligence. Her primary education came from "the streets"; her life has been checkered by many ups and downs. Her marriage was forced by her father; her husband later left her for a younger woman. After a while he returned, bringing his daughter by "the other woman" for Ttonggol Manshin to raise! At one point she set her pre-teen children up in the business of selling small black-market items, while she peddled vegetables from door to door.

She is not happy with her lot in life, even though she feels that she is conducting a necessary service. It wears her down both physically and mentally. By the description of her shamanizing activities, she even does the "knife-riding general" performance (See pp. 48-52). She claims that this is the most difficult of her kuts, leaving her filled with sadness, but she does it when necessary.

Ttonggol Manshin's husband is a perfect example of the Korean proverb: "A lazy, good-for-nothing man is (or becomes) a mudang's husband." Perhaps the culture shock of the Korean War broke her husband's spirit, for "an honest day's work" is something he just can't do. However, she still supports him and would not consider divorcing him. This husband never sits in on her kuts; he tries his utmost to avoid her customers.

Ttonggol Manshin charges only what the traffic will bear; she endeavors not to overcharge the poor. Her attitude brings to mind in some ways that of an old-fashioned "country doctor"; she helps everyone that she can.

Unlike many shamans, Ttonggol Manshin maintains good relations with her neighbors; she does not feel that being a shaman is the worst occupation for a woman. She would prefer that her daughters become shamans when they grow up rather than wine-house girls. Notwithstanding that statement, Ttonggol Manshin worries that her "possessing spirits" will occupy one of her daughters after she passes away. She feels that she fulfills a necessary function in life; besides, the spirits left her no choice in the matter after the spirit sickness (shinbyong).

Suwon Manshin

Suwon Manshin is perhaps the strangest of the three who will be listed here. Born in 1937 in Suwon, just south of the capital, she attended school in Seoul, returning home for holidays and vacations. While growing up, she was the spoiled darling of her teachers and parents, because she excelled in singing and acting. During her high school days, she had her own clique of friends, being one of the popular "bad girls" of her school.

She met her husband while in college and they were married very quickly after graduation due to the imminence of her pregnancy. Suwon Manshin did not fit into her husband's household because of its provincial background. The daughters-in-law were expected to be solicitous towards the parents, to enjoy cleaning, cooking and other household tasks. This did not suit Suwon Manshin at all, later causing trouble. She received nothing but contempt from her old-fashioned sister-in-law, who was the virtual ruler of the household. It was a great relief when her husband obtained a position in Seoul and they moved there.

Sometime after being baptized into the Catholic church, Suwon Manshin became "possessed," experiencing visions and premonitions. She predicted that a certain local police station would suffer a disaster; three days later it burned to the ground. Her brother gave her a bunch of sleeping pills (with the idea of overdosing her), but even taking the whole packet didn't kill her. So, she left her parent's home with the idea of becoming a mudang.

After a short time, she started to study Shamanism seriously, with an eye towards becoming the top mudang in Seoul. Later,

when a former classmate failed to contract her to perform a kut ensuring the success of her husband's business, Suwon Manshin felt completely crushed.

Suwon Manshin began with many great plans such as forming a mudang society, helping childless old people, and other ideas, but all have come to naught. She seems to have been motivated by personal gain rather than any other factor. She even attempted to ease out of her shaman role and become an entrepreneur, but she cannot quit shamanizing as it is her only reliable source of income. She said that whenever she needs to argue with a bill or tax collector, she assumes a masculine role, even though she doesn't want to.

Receiving advice about money, these two customers arrived in a chauffered car.

100

Social and Religious Conflicts

On a personal level, the role of the mudang does not seem to have changed drastically in Korea. They are still ranked in a low category, even by those people who use their services. A shaman's children suffer social ostracism; relatives consider themselves sunk in shame and try to hide their relation to a mudang.

Even though Korea is rapidly industrializing, and it is predicted that by 1990 the largest segment of its population will be Christians, it seems that enough people "believe" so that kosa and Chusok will continue in Korea for a long time to come.

Nor is it the poor and ignorant who use the services of a shaman. At Mount Samgak, almost every day he attended the author has seen expensive foreign cars parked outside, the chauffeur waiting, a well-dressed business man inside. Perhaps he wants a prediction about a business venture in Japan? One wealthy looking executive was seen to come out of the Mudang Headquarters wearing a St. Christopher medal. "Help is where you find it" has long been a human motto. Help from more than one source has long been a practice in Korea.

Faith Healing for Mental Illness Still Flourishing

According to a survey published in the *Korea Times* newspaper on March 10, 1983, a majority of Korea's protestant pastors still follow a Shamanistic attitude towards mental illness. A paper presented by two Seoul National University professors, Sohn Chin-uk and Lee Pu-yong, of its Medical College, emphasizes that protestant ministers in Korea believe that mental illness is "the work of devils" (80.6 percent), whereas Korea's Catholic priests recommend a psychiatrist or doctor. Mental illness within one's own family, was to be treated by "faith healing" among 65 percent of the protestant pastors. As for those who become mentally disturbed after a revival meeting or prayer session on a mountain top, 84.6 percent of the protestants regarded those people as "possessed by devils." Thus the Shamanistic attitude that the mentally ill are possessed by evil spirits seems to have passed over into Korea's protestant Christian movement.

Presently only a third of the protestant pastors support psychotherapy or medical therapy for mental illness, but two-thirds of the Catholic priests endorse this more modern method. The protestants explain that faith healing is more effective than other means, but perhaps this reflects on both the congregation and the pastors. It would seem that the Seoul National University's Medical College professors are trying to point out how pervasive is the influence of Shamanism in medicine, even today.

It would seem that protestant pastors who tell their congregational members, when pregnancy is imminent or birth prophesized, that daily attendance at 4:30 a.m. prayer meetings will produce healthy children, have somewhat taken over the role of Shamanist spirits. Until the noise abatement program became more strict, the 4:30 a.m. bells for prayer used amplifiers, and were common all over the Republic. Many a sermon within such churches still points out that calamity is due to "sin" on the part of the Christian household. Although the antecedents for such beliefs can be directly traced to John Calvin in the Western world, the general tenor seems similar to Shamanism.

In the United States there is a trend for protestant ministers to be trained in psychology in order to assist in counseling their parishioners. This still seems in Korea's future, for the women who have problems, especially in domestic matters, hesitate to consult a male pastor. It is easier to go to a female shaman, since her professional background reflects centuries of handling such problems. It would seem that it will be some time before shamans are forced out of business in Korea because there is no longer need for them.

It is a further interesting note that when missionaries translated the Christian scriptures into Korean, they chose the term "Hananim" to stand for "God." This is the Shamanist "Heavenly Spirit." His role is discussed at greater length in a companion volume to this one.

Spirit Marriages Arranged for KAL Plane Victims

Daily the newspapers contain references indicating that Shamanism is still very much alive in the hearts of Korea's average citizens, especially when meeting birth, death and major calamities. Due to the firm belief within Shamanism that the "soul" lives after death as a "spirit," the surviving relatives need to worry if a person meets accidental death... or dies without proper funeral ceremonies... or dies before having been married and producing children, since these are considered among the normal "joys" to which a human being is entitled. An unhappy spirit is liable to return and haunt the families, as discussed on pp. 63-66.

The victims of the Korean Air Lines atrocity were mourned by their families of a dozen nationalities, but Koreans who were relatives of unmarried young people had a special concern. A recent *Korea Herald* headline indicated the depths of worry over the fate of those souls who were not even engaged and yet were in their twenties. The parents felt a responsibility and blamed themselves for not having arranged marriages or at least engagements before tragedy struck.

Accordingly parents of four plane crash victims, two young ladies aged 23 and 24, both stewardesses on the fatal plane, were "engaged" by their parents in a ceremony to two young men who also died at the same time, age 27 and 24. After the "engagement ceremony," the two spirits will be "married" within 49 days. Korean Airlines officials helped in the arrangements, so as to soothe the "spirits" of these four young people. In one case, the parents met while visiting Hokkaido to search for plane wreckage. In the other case, the father asked KAL officials to find the name of a single female victim whose family would be agreeable to have their daughter's spirit marry the spirit of their son. These were not people whom one would ordinarily consider uneducated or superstitious. When looking deeply beneath the surface of Korean culture, one discovers its more sophisticated facade has been built upon the "will of the spirits."

Past and Present Related

It is noteworthy that the most thorough study of the role of Korean women in society, from ancient times to 1945, is now in English and edited by a Professor Kim Yung-chung on the faculty of Ewha Woman's University. This book commences its chapter titled "Lowborn Women of Influence" with a discussion of shamans. According to this one-volume abridgment of a three-volume work (*Han'guk yosong-sa*), all available statistics for the prevalence of females over males in the role of shamans run at least two-thirds to one-third, even during the period known as the Japanese Occupation. Furthermore, this book states that Queen Min's favorite shamaness, Chillyongun, had ready access to *both* King Kojong and Queen Min. This spirit-medium's son was given a high post, although ordinarily the children of the lowest class (chonmin) were not eligible.

In time of sickness within the royal household, until Western medicine arrived in the person of Dr. Horace Allen, the shamans were the first ones summoned. Not merely illness but a political crisis would necessitate consultation with shamans that so they could give a divination. This custom still prevails among a number of Korea's business men, although it may be done privately, without fanfare or publicity.

In any case, Seoul today is much more open to Shamanism than in the early Yi dynasty when the kings passed laws or regulations to prevent Buddhist monks and nuns, as well as shamans, from entering the capital city under pain of death. This law against Buddhist monastic orders held for centuries, and is rather well known, but the court relented against prohibiting mudang or paksu from entering because their services were so much in demand, even within the royal or noble circle.

Shamanism and Democracy

Korean Shamanism has been basically oriented, throughout the centuries, towards serving the individual, rather than involved with a large social unit. Furthermore, this religion did not promote or encourage architecture as a necessary place for holding large group meetings. Either the home itself or the mudang's tang was adequate for small sessions. When more than fifty people were involved, the ceremonies were normally held outdoors in the midst of nature, where the millenia-old deities would feel quite at home and could be more easily and directly addressed.

Neo-Confucianism, which remained Korea's official guiding faith for over 500 years, was both patriarchial and family-

Zo Zayong, director of the Emileh Museum, seen with Choi Hui-a, the first American *mudang*.

oriented, rather then matriarchal and individual-oriented as Shamanism tended to be. As the Republic moved further and further into a modernized, industrial economy, women came to occupy a more important social position and the nuclear family as a major unit gradually came to supplant the extended family system. All this happened during the twentieth century. Confucianism, which had postponed Korea's scientific advance compared with other powers, has found itself somewhat outmoded in many respects. A greater emphasis on individual worth has emerged in modern Korea, along with freedom of choice in religion, as assured by the Constitution.

As for the present political focus of Korean Shamanism, it is thoroughly anti-Communist. Many of the larger kut have dedicatory streamers emblazoned with anti-Communist slogans, or else display ribbons advocating unification of the peninsula without communization.

A wide streak of democracy runs throughout Korea's Shamanism as practiced in the Seoul area. For example, there exists, in a certain sense, only one Mountain Spirit, one San-shin, yet each mountain or good-sized foothill has its local deity and he is potent in that region. No feeling of jealousy or absolute hierarchy exists. In fact, outside of a vague, benign Heavenly Spirit, the deities of Shamanism are not rivals, as pointed out in the author's companion volume, *Shamanist Folk Paintings: Korea's Eternal Spirits* (just published by Hollym International). Each spirit has his or her special area of concern, where it can prove most beneficial or most potent in rooting out evils.

Therefore, when an attempt began in 1946-47 to Communize the northern part of the Korean peninsula, the manshin living there became very discontent. All who could manage, moved south as far as Seoul, when the opportunity presented itself with war's vicissitudes. The capital area already contained a basic core of the northern-type practioners, so the refugees from Communism blended in. The newcomers, not having lived under the heaviest pressure from the Japanese Occupation, carried an older form of worship, perhaps. The new immigrants from North Korea had been able to preserve more of their ancient Shamanist roots in regard to the ecstatic tradition.

The Fifth Republic

In 1980 the Fifth Republic began with a new constitution which, among other things, stressed the preservation of ancient cultural traditions without prejudice. Thus, under the presidency of Chun Doo-hwan, kuts have always been openly permitted. As this book goes to press, a large ritual is planned in honor of the Mountain Spirit, which will include prayers directed towards the peninsula's unification, in a democratic manner. A representative of the Blue House will be present to receive whatever "message from the gods" (presumably from the Mountain Spirit, who is related to the nation's progenitor, Tangun) is received by the manshin Oh Oh-hi, when she goes into ecstatic trance. (Her picture can be seen on the rear of the dust jacket.)

It seems a proper time for the government and Korean society at large to admit, without shame, the existence of Shamanism as a religion, instead of hiding it under a rug. It is both Korea's longest-lasting and most ancient religion. Much prejudice still clings from Confucian-tinted centuries, however. For example, scholars who compiled the latest unbridged dictionary (Korean-Korean) totally omitted the word "manshin," though including the less polite "mudang."

It has taken a long campaign by the author to have the "S" of "Shamanism" capitalized in English, in the same manner as the "C" is capitalized for Christianity and the "B" for Buddhism.

The Chinese character "man" used in "manshin" means "ten thousand." It is not an exact term, but really signifies "a great number." Since all human beings become "spirits" upon death, there are, as one Korean teacher of manshin solemnly assured this author, "now many billions of spirits in the ether."

8 THE FUTURE?

As more is written and known about Shamanistic symbolism, it will be easier for a larger public to appreciate the nuances of a performance. If not "believers," they

An eleven year-old girl, performing as the Generals of the Five Directions, with divining flags. She has not been "called" by the spirits but is practicing the steps of the ancient rituals as theatre.

may become "appreciative audience" for this religious psycho-drama. The biggest problem seems to be how to retain the authenticity when kut become more and more of a tourist attraction, as they surely will. Perhaps the government, which not long ago banned kuts, will now have to offer guidance and protection.

The Littlest Mudang

Concerning what kind of persons will become shamans in Korea's future, in 1981 the author saw a kut performed outdoors at the Mudang Headquarters in the shadow of its huge natural rock. The star attraction was a twelve-year old manshin who had been "called by the spirits" at the age of

six. She not only rode the knives for the generals, but leaped several feet in the air above them, dancing rapidly on the blades.

First she licked the knife blade's sharp edge with her tongue. It seems that the "spirits" never rest in their search for a medium to serve as their interpreter. At the close, this girl was performing a kut for the sake of the unification of the Korean peninsula. Perhaps she will have better luck than the politicians!

105

SUGGESTED FURTHER READINGS

Edward B. Adams, *Through the Gates of Seoul.* (Two Volumes) Seoul: Sahm-Bo Publishing, 1971.

Isabella Bird Bishop, *Korea and Her Neighbors.* (reprint) Seoul: Yonsei University Press, 1970.

Joseph Campbell, *The Masks of God: Oriental Mythology.* London: Specker & Warburg, 1962.

Yun-Shik Chang, "Shamanism as Folk Existentionalism." ASPAC QUARTERLY, Winter, 1981.

Anthony Christie, *Chinese Mythology.* London: Paul Hamlyn Publishing, 1968.

Jon Carter Covell, *Korea's Cultural Roots.* Seoul: Hollym Corporation, 1981.

_____, *Korea's Buddhist Temples.* Korea National Tourist Commission, 1982.

Marcea Eliade, *Shamanism: Archaic Techniques of Ecstacy.* translated by William Trask, Princeton: Princeton University Press, 1964.

Youngsook Kim Harvey, *Six Korean Women: The Socialization of Shamans.* St. Paul, West Publishing, 1978.

Ilyon, *Samguk Yusa.* translated by Tae Hung Ha & Grafton Mintz, Seoul: Yonsei University Press, 1972.

Wanne J. Joe, *Traditional Korea: A Cultural History.* Seoul: Chungang University Press, 1973.

Tong Ni Kim, *Ulhwa the Shaman: A Novel of Korea and Three Stories.* translated by Ahn Jung Ho, New York: Larchwood Press, 1978.

Jung Young Lee, *Korea Shamanistic Rituals,* The Hague, Paris and New York: Mouton Publishers, 1983

Legeza Laszlo, *Tao Magic.* New York: Random House, 1975.

Andreas Lommel, *Shamanism: The Beginning of Art.* Toronto: McGraw-Hill, (c/o date unknown).

Sandra Mattielli, (ed.) *Virtues in Conflict.* Seoul: Samhwa Publications, 1977.

Henry N. Michael, *Studies in Siberian Shamanism.* (reprint) Toronto: University of Toronto Press, 1972.

Zdena Novotna (ed.) *The Monkey King.* translated by Goerge Theiner, London: Hamlyn Publishers, 1964.

Edward H. Schaffer, *Ancient China.* New York: Time-Life Books, 1967.

C.A.S. Williams, *Outlines of Chinese Symbolism and Art Motives.* (reprint) New York: Dover Publications, 1976.

Zayong Zo, *Diamond Mountains.* (Two Volumes) Seoul: Emileh Museum Press, 1975.

_____, *Folkism.* Emileh Museum Press, 1970.

_____, *Guardians of Happiness: Shamanistic Tradition in Korean Folk Painting,* Seoul: Emileh Museum Press, 1982.

_____, *Korean Folk Painting.* Seoul: 1977.

_____, *Spirit of the Korean Tiger.* Seoul: Emileh Museum Press, 1972.

INDEX

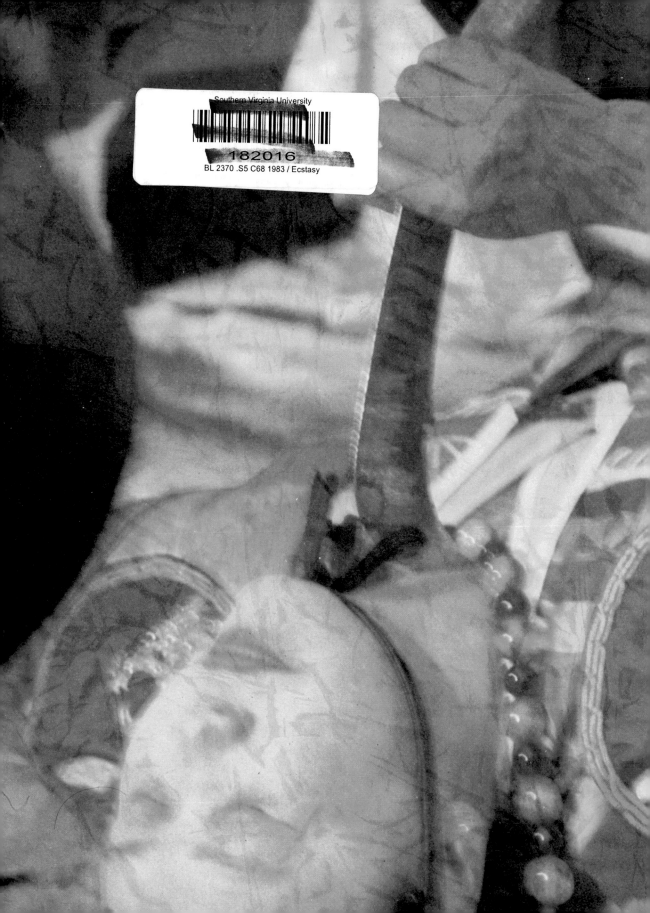